CLASSICAL INTERIORS

Historical and Contemporary

ELIZABETH MEREDITH DOWLING

New York · Paris · London · Milan

To my family—

Geddes, Meredith, Michael,

Edward, Lucy,

Charles, Arthur

First published in the United States of America in 2013 by
Rizzoli International Publications, Inc.
300 Park Avenue South
New York, NY 10010
www.rizzoliusa.com

ISBN: 978-0-8478-4099-1
LCCN: 2013939434

Designed by Abigail Sturges

Distributed to the U.S. trade by Random House, New York

Printed and bound in China

2013 2014 2015 2016 2017 / 10 9 8 7 6 5 4 3 2 1

[PAGE 2] *One of the twin pilasters that frame either side of the altar of St. James' Goose Creek Church, Berkeley County, South Carolina, c. 1707–19. These are considered the earliest examples in America of Composite capitals.*

[PAGE 5] *Living room detail, Georigan Revival House, Lexington, Kentucky, designed by Fairfax & Sammons Architects*

[PAGE 6] *Entry foyer, Williamstrip Pool Pavilion, Gloucestershire, England, designed by Craig Hamilton Architects*

CONTENTS

ACKNOWLEDGMENTS

The author and the publisher gratefully acknowledge the generous contribution of Richard H. Driehaus to this book.

Many individuals assisted in the formation and presentation of the great variety of classicism represented in this book. I would first like to thank Robin H. Prater for approaching this project with energy and dedication in locating illustrations that present the beauty of past architecture; Dr. Richard John for his suggestions of rare books and sources of sixteenth-century engravings; Myke Clifford for research and re-creation of images from rare books; Pamela Huntington Darling for her personal introduction to excellent classical firms in France; Francis Terry for his effort to realize the first publication of Hanover Lodge; Allan Greenberg for giving so many young architects a firm basis for their design thoughts and helping me understand both his work and that of his many students; Marc Appleton for his generous access to his work and design philosophy; Sir Donald Insall and Nicholas Thompson for clarifying the care of old buildings in Britain; Pilar Molyneux for taking great interest in this project and for giving generously of her time, including tours of projects; Craig Hamilton for the generosity of a personal tour of his projects and explanation of their relationship to his philosophy of design; Mary Miers for her help with historic *Country Life* images. To the individuals who took such care in making this book a special representation of current classical design, I would especially like to thank Nina Bransfield, Justin Detwiler, Peter Dixon, Dawn Fritz, Laure Jakobiak, Neil McKenna, Gail Tomlinson, John Vernon, and Peter Walker.

[OPPOSITE] *Juan Pablo Molyneux introduced an axis from the Chinese Hall through the grand salon ending in the library in the hôtel particulier Claude Passart, Paris.*

CHAPTER ONE

SURVEY OF CLASSICAL INTERIOR DESIGN

ELIZABETH MEREDITH DOWLING

[1.1] *Renzo Mongiardino's countless painted effects include trompe l'oeil marble, parquet, and inlays.* Reprinted with permission of *House Beautiful* © 1993

[1.2] *For a dining room on Manhattan's Upper East Side designed by Molyneux Studios, muralist Anne Harris covered the four walls with a narrative inspired by Bartholomäus Strobel's* Saint John the Baptist Beheaded. Museo Nacional del Prado

[1.3 OPPOSITE] *Inspired by the palaces of the Renaissance, Italian designer Renzo Mongiardino created a fantasy of a reading room for the late Peter Sharp of Manhattan. It is meant to simulate a rooftop terrace, with trompe l'oeil pilasters framing visionary views of the city skyline. The center desk was modeled after a design by Michelangelo.* Reprinted with permission of *House Beautiful* © 1993

Architecture expresses meaning through the vocabulary of its details (fig. 1.1). It communicates through color, rhythm, shadow, material, proportion, and scale. Buildings give three dimensions to abstract concepts; for example, democracy is visualized through the syntax of a Greek temple in the Lincoln Memorial. All architecture speaks, but, like writing, some of its authors are eloquent while others are less articulate. Classical architecture employs a rich language developed across twenty-five centuries and many cultures. This is a language of details understood worldwide with its powerful vocabulary of subtle nuance and inflection.

Within the study of architectural history, the subject of classical interiors has garnered a minor position in the coverage of twentieth-century design, as has the general subject of classical architecture after the 1930s. Writers and

[1.4] *Comparison of the Doric, Ionic, and Corinthian orders drawn by Sheldon Kostelecky while a graduate student at the University of Notre Dame*

historians have devoted their attention instead to the myriad new approaches to the aesthetic of simplicity that developed with the focus on machine- and technology-inspired design dating from the Bauhaus era of the 1920s. The rush to new forms, materials, systems, and philosophy created an antipathy toward traditional and classical design. Rather than embracing diversity, modernism shunned the ancestry of the architectural profession, preferring instead to see their roots as shallow and made of steel.

The introduction of the new style of simplicity was excitingly shocking in its appearance, but the focus on dematerialization has limits. The contrast of simplicity, for many, offers less fascination than the delights of complexity. This aspect of modernism has been covered in immense detail by many authors, and what this book sets as its goal is the coverage of the other face of the present: the spirited pursuit of beauty inspired by the human form and human history. In any group of designers there will be ideological purists who shun all but a certain form of design, but this book seeks to explore the variety encompassed within classical and traditional design. The work of these selected designers and architects represent an approach that demands skill and knowledge of both the profession and the history of the profession. The artistry of craftspeople demonstrates individuality and skill rather than the perfection of factory production. The incorporation of permanent art in the form of murals and carving is evident throughout the selected works (fig. 1.2). Interior design is the most fragile of all aspects of architecture. It is subject to changing fashion and to the tastes of owners. This book explores the architecture of the interior rather than its most temporal elements, the impermanent aspects of furniture and art objects. Many of the selected structures display elegant and important furnishings

and, where appropriate, these will be described, but the focus remains on the spaces and their enclosure by thoughtfully detailed surfaces. Unfortunately, the accompanying photographs only hint at the beauty of the spaces; to be fully understood, architecture, as a three-dimensional art, must be experienced. Renzo Mongiardino (1916–1998; fig. 1.3) referred to during his career as the world's greatest living interior decorator,[1] wrote of the changeable aspect of interiors:

> Unlike the facade of a house or a church, and unlike a painting or a sculpture, the view of a room lies precisely in its hollow form, at the center of its four walls. In the room, a person is surrounded by the walls; light—the light of morning, of afternoon, and of evening, the artificial lights of night—transforms everything. In the morning the room is ignited by the sun, with strong shadows; in the afternoon it is softened; at dawn, cold; toward evening, gilded; and then, ashine with the blaze of nighttime lights. Every object, material, painting, bronze, piece of furniture will be involved in the process, and every room will have its most beautiful hour.[2]

To fully appreciate the excellence of twenty-first century traditional design, this book sets its context with a succinct review of the history of classical architecture—its origins and revivals.[3] This brief review of the ancestry of classical form will awaken interest in some readers and reacquaint others with elements that enhance the appreciation of beautiful architecture.[4] The pursuit of beauty through the language of its details is a primary aim of classicists, and its important function is addressed in David Watkin's essay "Ornament: A Source of Beauty." Education in the history of architecture will be addressed in two essays. Carol A. Hrvol Flores presents the "Grand Tour" in its eighteenth-century context, and I present

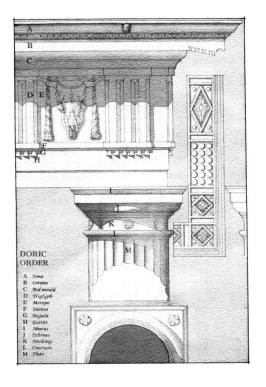

DORIC ORDER
A Sima
B Corona
C Bed mould
D Triglyph
E Metope
F Taenia
G Regula
H Guttae
I Abacus
J Echinus
K Necking
L Cincture
M Flute

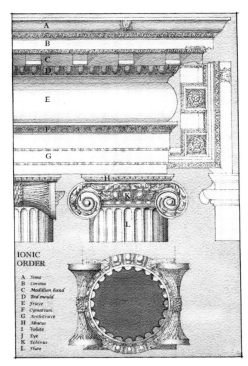

IONIC ORDER
A Sima
B Corona
C Modillion band
D Bed mould
E Frieze
F Cymatium
G Architrave
H Abacus
I Volute
J Eye
K Echinus
L Flute

CORIN-
THIAN
ORDER
A Sima
B Corona
C Modillion
D Bed mould
E Dentil band
F Frieze
G Cymatium
H Abacus
I Fleuron
J Lip
K Calathos
L Helices
M Volute
N Cauliculus
O Cincture
P Flute

current classical architectural education. The final essay, by Richard Sammons, explores proportion—the unseen armature of classical design. Portfolios of the work of selected contemporary architects and designers are interspersed between the essays. The diversity of current classicism is evident in this exemplary work. The presentation of current work begins with the subject of historic preservation and restoration. To understand current classicism, one must not forget the effects of mid-twentieth-century modernism on the loss of skilled building crafts. The renewed demand for fine carpentry, stone and wood carvers, plasterers, muralists, and iron workers first occurred through reconstruction of war-damaged and storm-ravaged buildings followed soon after by patrons' desire for new construction. Selected work of four firms demonstrate the ability of both designers and artists to worthily repair and adapt surviving classical buildings for present use.

GREEK AND ROMAN FOUNDATIONS OF CLASSICAL ARCHITECTURE

The first classical building no longer exists. Opinions of scholars differ on the origin of the details of what became known as classical architecture, but their refined development in Greece is not in question. Details like fluted columns existed in Egypt, but it was in the Peloponnese and the Aegean Islands that they reached their ultimate form. Greek civilization prized the homes of their gods above earthly dwellings, and the temple and its elements were refined across centuries in such a manner that the parts remain as the foundation of the most intricately developed architectural language any culture has produced. The basic unit of classical design is the column and the beam it supports—which in architectural parlance is the "order." Three principal orders were used with enough frequency and consistency to be identified with geographic and ethnic areas of Greece and its colonies (fig. 1.4). The aggressive Dorian race spread across a wide area from Sicily to Sparta and Crete. They created a set of details that Vitruvius, a Roman architect and writer from the first century BCE, referred to as Doric. The Greeks of Asia Minor contributed the Ionic order, and the Corinthian order first appears at the Temple of Apollo at Bassae in southern Greece.

Vitruvius (c. 80–c. 15 BCE) created the first comprehensive book on architecture in antiquity, or, perhaps, the only one to survive (fig. 1.5). His *Ten Books of Architecture (De Architectura* in Latin) remains in print two thousand years after being handwritten on scrolls. It contains information of continuing importance to the fields of urban planning and ecological design, but most especially to setting out the details of classical architecture. The contents of his book were revered by Renaissance architects, who visually comprehended the unillustrated text through his words; however, it is now known that his work was a polemic on appropriate design, not a mere record of the methods of his own era. He wrote of complex issues with moderate clarity, recorded the names of the orders, and implied their association with gender. This information defining the elements of the orders and referencing gender was especially influential on the implementation of antique details in later design.

GENDER AND PROPORTION OF THE ORDERS

Gender identification with the orders is an intriguing association of the column with the human body. Except for the Greek Doric, whose shaft rises boldly from its platform, columns have heads, bodies, and feet—capital, shaft, and base. Vitruvius also implied they had sexual identity. These ideas originated in Greece, and Vitruvius, unlike many later Renaissance theorists, likely traveled in Greece and observed the buildings he referenced. Of the three primary Greek orders, the Doric column represents the solid proportions of the male; the Ionic, somewhat more slender and more detailed, represents the adult female; and the Corinthian, the tallest and most elaborate, represents the youthful female (figs. 1.6, 7). Although current design does not reference gods and goddesses, the anthropomorphism of gender presents viable clues to creating an appropriate character for an interior. Stoic and severe, modest and plain, ornate and spirited—classical detailing presents a malleable range of personality for architecture.

Vitruvius, however, presented gender in terms of a column's appropriateness in expressing the innate character of a particular god or goddess. His reference to these ideas was an attempt to guide Romans in determining the proper representation for a temple dedicated to a particular god. Vitruvius admired the reserve of Hellenic design and he wished

to reform his countrymen's overwhelming preference for the ornate and to encourage intellectual, rather than emotional, choices. But it appears he was unsuccessful. A temple from Vitruvius's era, the period of Augustus, constructed to represent Mars, employed the Corinthian order (fig. 1.8). The effeminate aspect of the order, with its beautiful tendrils and acanthus leaves, represented the origin of Mars from the fertilization of his mother, Juno, by a

[1.8] *An engraving re-creating a Corinthian capital from the Temple of Mars Ultor, Rome, by Hector D'Espouy for* Fragments d'architecture antique

moldings are matched with flat fillets; some reach upward, some downward for support. All are essential elements; all have their function, and together produce the beauty of classical architecture.[5] A further discussion of moldings can be found in David Watkin's essay on beauty and ornament.

The height of columns is a proportional relationship, and Vitruvius employs multiples of the base diameter as a means of describing their differ-

flower. But Augustus changed the focus of the god's character by dedicating the temple to Mars Ultor—Mars the Avenger of the death of his ancestor Julius Caesar. The new temple became important to members of the military, but the use of the Corinthian, rather than the more severe and manly Doric, indicates a preference for the elegance of the composition over the theoretical projection of an interpretable representation of their deity of war. Architects would adhere to Vitruvian ideas of propriety only upon the Renaissance rediscovery of his writing.

Also contained in *The Ten Books of Architecture* are proportional prescriptions for the height of columns and the numerous moldings that compose the columns and their beams, as well as other requisite ornamental details like the metopes and triglyphs of the Doric frieze (fig. 1.9). Curving

ing heights. The Doric is the most solid, with a proportion of one diameter at its base to six diameters in height. In Book IV, he describes the reasoning behind the Greek Doric in anthropomorphic terms of size and gender:

> On finding that in a man, the foot was one sixth of the height, they applied the same principle to the column, and reared the shaft, including the capital, to a height six times its thickness at its base. Thus the Doric column, as used in buildings, began to exhibit the proportions, strength, and beauty of the body of a man.[6]

Vitruvius's next discussion provided similar information for the Ionic order (fig. 1.10) and related the column to a female deity, thus attaching an interpretation of gender and columnar form that would be of great significance to architects from the Renaissance to the present:

[1.9] *Louis-Philippe-Francois Boitte (1820–1906), watercolor showing a reconstructed view of the east facade of the Parthenon designed by Ichtinos and Callicrates (447–438 BCE)*

[1.10] *Temple of Athena Nike/Apteros (c. 420 BCE) constructed on a precipice guarding the path to the Propylaea, or gateway, of the Acropolis. Callicrates, who along with Ichtinos designed the Parthenon, here created a tetrastyle Ionic temple honoring Athena as the goddess of Victory.*

[1.11] *In scenes of the destruction of Troy, a Temple of Athena is depicted with thinly attenuated Ionic columns. Red-figure ceramic volute-krater, Apulian Late Classical, attributed to the Baltimore Painter, c. 340–330 BCE.* Michael C. Carlos Museum, Carlos Collection of Ancient Art

Just so afterwards, when they desired to construct a temple to Diana in a new style of beauty, they translated these footprints into terms characteristic of the slenderness of women, and thus made a column the thickness of which was only one eighth of its height, so that it might have a taller look. At the foot they substituted the base in place of a shoe; in the capital they placed the volutes, hanging down at the right and left like curly ringlets, and ornamented its front with cymatia and with festoons of fruit arranged in place of hair, while they brought the flutes down the whole shaft, falling like the folds in the robes worn by matrons. Thus in the invention of the two different kinds of columns, they borrowed manly beauty, naked and unadorned, for the one, and for the other the delicacy, adornment, and proportions characteristic of women.[7]

Proportion dominates the design of classical architecture from the smallest molding to the spacing of a range of columns. The proportional relationships are not absolute but change over time and shape the expression of an individual architect. The language of classical architecture is immensely flexible, as can be seen when comparing such architecture as the delicacy of the eighteenth-century work of Robert Adam with the stoic quality of fifth-century Greece. Richard Sammons's essay on proportion illuminates the unseen armature of classical design.

Further details worth noting reflect the depth to which Greek architects understood the need to alter substance in order to convey proper appearance. In the abstract, columns are cylinders; however, if made in this simple geometric

[1.12] *Temple of Hera I, Paestum, Italy (second half of the sixth century BCE). The flanking colonnade of this archaic temple in the Greek colony located in southern Italy shows an extreme shaping of the column shaft and a widely flaring echinus of the column capital. Entasis first appeared at the Temple of Hera I, and, in succeeding centuries, these details gradually change from squat proportions with bold curvature of the column shaft to the subtle curvature of the Parthenon columns with a proportion of base diameter to height of 1:5.5 and a barely visible entasis of ¹¹⁄₁₆ inches of outward curvature of the shaft.*

shape, as often occurs with modern concrete work, the result is lifeless and mechanical. Greek column shafts have two further refinements: attenuation and entasis. The first, attenuation, is always used in classical design (fig. 1.11). The second, entasis, is the ultimate perfection of a column and is less often employed. Attenuation is the diminishing diameter of the column from its largest size at the base to its smallest at the neck or top of the shaft. Specific effects of solidity to delicacy can be created with the degree of attenuation employed in each column design. Entasis is a slight bulging of the column to prevent the outside lines of the shaft from appearing to curve inwards (fig. 1.12). Greek architects employed this detail on the Parthenon and note of it was made by Vitruvius:

With regard to the enlargement that is added to the middle of columns, which among the Greeks is called . . . [entasis], at the end of the book a figure and calculation will be added, showing how it can produce an agreeable and appropriate appearance.[8]

Most unfortunately, no illustrations survived in any copies of Vitruvius's writing. Exactly how entasis was achieved is still the subject of conjecture; however, the enlargement in Greek architecture results in the shape of an ellipse. Roman architects employed a simpler method of adjusting straight lines to give the appearance of a slight bulge.[9] Such refinements as entasis were difficult to achieve with hand tools, and the extreme desire for visual perfection is one reason Greek aesthetics is afforded enduring respect.

[1.13] *Although inaccurate in many details like the inclusion of clerestory windows, this reconstruction of the interior of the Parthenon in a nineteenth-century engraving by E. Thiersch is a lively presentation of the spectacular chryselephantine (ivory and gold) statue of Athena created by the sculptor Phidias. The wide interior was made specifically to receive this approximately 40-foot-tall statue. The superimposed Doric columns provide a backdrop for the statue and a second level to view the magnificent work of art.*

Greek civic life was less complex than that of the later Romans with their vast empire encompassing numerous cultures. The variety of Roman public architecture reflects this difference. In architecture, the Greeks' most lasting contribution to architecture was through the increasing refinement of their temples. Immense effort and the finances of Greek city-states produced buildings that later defined classical architecture. From the earliest temples of the seventh century BCE to the Hellenistic temples of the second century BCE, plans with central rooms surrounded by a colonnade predominated with previously mentioned details occurring in most, but not all, temples. The Parthenon (447–432 BCE) represents the remarkable ability of a culture to produce a monument that will for all time signify greatness in artistic accomplishment (fig. 1.13). Construction of the Parthenon was directed by the Athenian ruler Pericles, who wished to restore the political position of Athens as well as repair the physical damage inflicted by the Persians upon the sacred precinct of the Acropolis. Architects Ictinus and Callicrates created a subtle new temple design to receive the immense forty-foot-tall gold-and-ivory cult statue of Athena sculpted by Phidias. The new design combined sculptural elements of the Ionic with a more delicate Doric order, producing a new interpretation of the goddess as the virginal Athena Parthenos and advancing Pericles' desire to bring about an alliance of the Dorian and Ionian people. The new interior plan offered increased space for the cult statue and gave it a backdrop of superimposed Doric columns. Because width of column base and height are proportionally related, two levels of columns allowed for more generous interior space. Single columns of the height required would have filled the space with columns of immense width, leaving little circulation space. Although the building may appear to be a composition of simple geometric forms, visual refinements adjusted elements to appear more perfect to our eyes. Apparently level surfaces curve upwards to prevent the appearance of sagging that we perceive in long level lines. The axes of the columns tilt inward, column spacing varies, and sculpture leans forward. These refinements give the composition a sense of life and buoyancy and all are extremely difficult devices to accomplish with hand labor and simple tools. Each of the refinements is incorporated in other temples, but only at the Parthenon are all devices employed together, testifying to the overwhelming desire to display the greatness of Athens through their new temple.[10]

ROMAN CIVIC ARCHITECTURE

Roman civilization produced exceptional architecture for many new cultural necessities and did so with the added innovation of arcuated construction. The starting point, as so often, was the Roman admiration for Greek culture. As the Roman Empire expanded to encompass Greece and her colonies, the conquerors adopted the construction details of the Doric, Ionic, and Corinthian orders. The Romans themselves contributed two orders to the vocabulary of classical design: the Tuscan and the Composite orders (fig.1.14). The Tuscan is the most severe and elementary columnar form and was developed for the temples of the Etruscan people—one of the ancestral races that formed the Roman character. At the opposite end of the scale of architectural refinement was the Composite, a columnar creation commemorating the reign of the Emperor Titus (39–81 CE, reigning 79–81 CE). The base and shaft are the same as those of the Corinthian and Ionic columns, but the capital combines the defining elements of both orders—the curving volute from the Ionic and the layers of acanthus leaves from the Corinthian. Created for the Triumphal Arch of Titus, the Composite order symbolized imperial authority in the conquest of other cultures. The elements of classical architecture were employed in all

[1.14] *The Arch of Titus in Rome, c. 82 CE, memorializes the triumphant procession through Rome in 71 CE of Titus and his father Emperor Vespasian following their capture of Jerusalem in 70 CE. Sponsored by Titus's brother Domitian, the arch incorporated the earliest known examples of the Composite order that symbolizes imperial domination.*

[1.15] *The back-to-back cellae of the Temple of Venus and Rome depicted in a restoration drawing by Léon Vaudoyer (1830) and published in* Fragments d'architecture antique *under the direction of Hector D'Espouy (undated).* Kenan Research Center—Atlanta History Center

[1.16] *The original interior appearance of the Pantheon is preserved in Giovanni Paolo Panini's* Interior of the Pantheon, Rome *(c. 1734). The hemispherical interior is accented with twenty-eight rows of coffers that lighten the effect of the massive concrete dome. The solitary light piercing through the oculus paints the surface in ever changing brilliance.* Samuel H. Kress Collection, image courtesy of National Gallery of Art, Washington, D.C., oil on canvas

Roman work, but two building forms represent their highest achievement in design: the temple and the imperial bath.

At first glance, Roman temples appear similar to Greek temples, since both are faced with a row of columns supporting a triangular pediment. From a distant corner view, they also appear to have a colonnade surrounding all sides of the building like Greek temples, but upon close inspection, the columns in Roman temples are frequently attached to three sides of the cella wall, providing a more spacious interior.[11] The Emperor Hadrian (76–138 CE, reigning 117–38 CE), a dedicated Hellenophile and architect, experimented with temple forms. His unique design for the temple of Amor and Roma (Venus and Rome) was a palindrome of back-to-back cellae that reflected the goddesses' names. The interior was likely vaulted, although only the apsidal end survives today

(fig. 1.15). Fortunately, Hadrian's most important contribution to architecture does survive in excellent condition due to continued use and maintenance through the centuries. This temple, the Pantheon (118–28 CE), is a spatial achievement made possible by Roman greatness in engineering. From the Etruscans, Romans learned to make true arches of stone. Combined with experimentation in the use of concrete, Romans created vaults and domes of great variety. Ever increasing spans allowed new spatial architecture never before known and hardly equaled since the second century. The Pantheon is the most significant surviving Roman temple and the most atypical, but its breathtaking beauty influenced generations of designers (fig. 1.16). The circular temple spans approximately 142 feet—a distance never again equaled in concrete and the greatest span of any type until

the fifteenth century with the construction of the slightly larger masonry dome of the Florence Cathedral.

The Pantheon grafts a traditional pediment temple facade upon the wall of a curving cylinder that encases the internal coffered dome. A symbolic sphere could be inscribed within as the dome rises to the height of its width. Dedicated to all the gods, the sphere of the building represents the curving vault of the heavens. The original approach to the building carried the visitor through a tight axial courtyard that diminished any view of the building beyond the traditional temple face. The unanticipated volume of space must have amazed ancient visitors even more than current visitors who know that an immense space awaits them. The walls and floors are covered with squares and circles rendered in stone of white, green, yellow, gray, and deep red. Columns of *giallo antico* and red porphyry appear in the lower level. Pilasters of red porphyry originally surrounded the interior in the upper attic zone, but these were replaced in 1747 by large panels giving a less appropriate larger scale to the details of this zone. Later, one bay was again restored to its original appearance.[12]

ROMAN BATHS

The bath as a facet of Roman life encompassed far more than the personal desire for cleanliness. In fact, entertainment was the principal aim of the great imperial thermae. Baths existed in larger family homes, but public baths could be found in small towns and grew in popularity and size in major cities. A census in Rome at the time of Agrippa in 33 BCE listed 170 baths and a later census in the fifth century CE recorded 856 baths.[13] Well past the glorious days of the Roman Empire, the baths in Rome continued to operate until barbarian invaders destroyed the aqueducts that provided the essential water from the surrounding countryside. The function of bathing developed from a necessity during the Repub-

lican period of Rome's history into a time-consuming and pleasurable activity in the Imperial Age. The activity, however, was highly democratic and was enjoyed by all no matter what economic or social status or gender (fig. 1.17). The first bath buildings included a few rooms with warm and cool pools, but over time the activity developed complex rituals with rooms for massage, application of oils, exercise, light swimming, hot baths, and dry heated rooms. This diversity of activities resulted in the creation of architecturally complex structures to house the many diversions of the bath. The bath building proper was situated within an immense garden that included areas for athletics and contemplation. The entire composition was bounded by a perimeter that housed rooms for libraries and classrooms.

Because the baths fell into disrepair after the barbarian invasions of the sixth century, only the Baths of Diocletian (298–305 CE) retain sufficient interior spaces to reveal the grandeur of Roman imperial architecture (fig. 1.18). The complex covered an area of approximately thirty acres closely following the general layout of the Baths of Caracalla constructed ninety years earlier; however, the later bath building itself was the largest ever constructed.[14] The main building covered a vast area of 785 feet by 485 feet.[15] The bilateral organization of the imperial baths exerted enormous influence on the imaginations of later generations of architects who came to Rome to study the ruins and draw inspiration for their own compositions. Through measured drawings and site sketches, architects returned home to create everything from train stations to government centers based on the bath organization. Many portions of the Baths of Diocletian survive, but the space most telling of imperial grandeur is the main frigidarium that was reconfigured by Michelangelo in 1563, some 1,200 years after its construction, to create the church of Santa Maria degli Angeli. This great hall's original eight red granite columns survive intact, giving the impression of support for the groin-vaulted ceiling. The original composition

[1.17] *Sir Lawrence Alma-Tadema, A Favourite Custom, 1909, oil on wood. This carefully researched but imaginative scene of the pleasures of the bath is set in the Stabian baths at Pompeii. Knowing the baths only through black-and-white photographs, the artist enriched the bath by adding marble floors and walls.* © Tate, London

[1.18 FOLLOWING PAGES] *In the fifth century invading Goths destroyed the Roman aqueducts and, without a source of water, the Baths of Diocletian ceased to function. At the bequest of Pope Pius IV in 1561, Michelangelo created a brilliant plan converting the frigidarium of the baths into the main sanctuary of the church of Santa Maria degli Angeli. The original vaults and 46-foot-tall red granite columns survive.*

included sequences of shaped spaces aligned on a cross axis. The vista stretched the full length of the building, broken only by screens of columns. Light entered from above through arched windows. The surfaces would have been covered by frescoes, the walls and floors by plaques of colored marbles. The astonishing beauty of the interiors can be appreciated to a degree by imagining the immense space of the bath looking similar to the ornamented interior of a building such as the eleventh-century Basilica of St. Mark in Venice, which continued the decorative tradition of marble-covered walls, patterned floors, and glowing ceiling mosaics. The carefully rendered re-creation views of the baths by the nineteenth-century architect Edmond Paulin provide a view of the space with the addition of the 3,000 bathers that was said to be the capacity of the building (fig. 1.19).

GREEK AND ROMAN HOUSES

In Book VI of his *Ten Books of Architecture*, Vitruvius addressed the Greek house and the Roman house, the latter being so well known to later periods through the excavations in Pompeii and Herculaneum. He begins his exposition on houses, however, with a polemic on the necessity of considering site and climate when designing a house. The detailed knowledge of sunlight and regional response to heating or cooling allowed the Romans to create houses of immense comfort and beauty (fig. 1.20). In the houses of the wealthiest citizens, comfort was achieved through a central heating system known as a hypocaust, which used hot air rising through clay ducts to heat the walls and floors. The urban house presented an unadorned face to the street and focused inwardly on a sequence of columned courts, or atria, that opened to the sky. Their sizes differed according to the magnitude of the house and its geographic location. The largest columned courtyard, the peristyle, was placed deep within the house.

[1.19] *Edmond Paulin (1848–1915) created numerous reconstructed drawings of the Baths of Diocletian like this fanciful cutaway view of the frigidarium and natatio depicting bathers taking advantage of the cool baths and open-air swimming.*

SURVEY OF CLASSICAL INTERIOR DESIGN

31

[1.20] *Through the rediscovery of Pompeii in 1748 and subsequent excavations, knowledge of the Roman house's plan and decoration served as inspiration for many nineteenth-century artists of historically themed paintings. Luigi Bazzani (1836–1927) created* A Pompeian Interior, *1882, displaying the atrium of a house with its impluvium to collect rainwater. Colorful frescoes decorate the walls and ceiling, and delicate furniture and fine Roman sculpture complete the image of the elegant life of the ancient Romans.* © Dahesh Museum of Art, oil on panel

Its row of columned passages surrounded an internal garden, often enlivened with fruit trees, flowers, and water. This form of inward-looking house worked magnificently for an urban setting providing privacy, security, and a buffer to the noise, dirt, and smells of the street. In addition to carefully rendered architectural details, walls were ornamented with frescoes containing references to religious or mythic subjects, expanding space into imaginary scenes or imitating fine materials. Except for a few examples like the well-preserved scenes in the Villa of the Mysteries in Pompeii, the finest Roman frescoes decorate the walls of museums today.

Although no early Greek houses survive intact, an extraordinary house, Villa Kérylos, inspired by its owner's study of ancient Greece, gives an idea of the delightful possibilities of life on the Mediterranean (figs. 1.21–24). In 1902, Theodore Reinach, an archaeologist, employed the architect Emmanuel Pontremoli to assist in realizing his dream of a home that provided a realistic backdrop for his studies of antiquity. The house is centered on a peristyle of twelve Doric columns of pure white Carrara marble. The walls are covered in representative frescoes, and the furniture and art objects are reproduced from items in museums in Naples, Munich, and London.[16]

DECLINE OF THE ROMAN EMPIRE

At its height of power under the Emperor Trajan (53–117 CE, reigning 98–117 CE), the Roman Empire extended to Britain to the west, northern Africa to the south, close to the Caspian Sea to the east, and as far as the borders of Austria and Hungary to the north. This swath of western and eastern Europe was essentially peaceful and enjoyed the comforts of Roman civilization; however, by the fourth century, the center of power and wealth had moved eastward, with Rome losing its position as the capital of the empire. The *Pax Romana* that had shaped the world for almost two hundred years was replaced with local centers of power that could not protect the populace from the

[1.22 TOP LEFT] *As in ancient Greek houses, the peristyle of the Villa Kérylos is the center of the design. Open to the sky, the courtyard roof is supported on twelve Carrara marble columns and the walls are covered with frescoes and mosaics depicting mythical scenes.*

[1.23 TOP RIGHT] *The ground-floor hall of the Villa Kérylos includes furniture based on examples of ancient Greek chairs in the National Archaeological Museum in Naples.*

[1.24 BOTTOM] *The octagonal triclinium, or dining room, of the Villa Kérylos, with reclining couches around the three tables.*

[1.25] *The bath of Villa Kérylos is inspired by Roman public baths in Pompeii. The octagonal pool is made of Carrara marble and is surrounded by four Ionic columns.*

incursion of barbarian tribes including the Huns, Visigoths, and Vandals. The extent of the empire decreased, ultimately surviving in the east under the name of the Byzantine Empire and, in its final decline, encompassing only the city of Constantinople, which in turn fell to the Ottoman Empire in 1453. In the west, historians generally accept the year 476 as the ultimate end of the Roman Empire. Without the provision of peace, culture declined throughout Western Europe. Architecture requires complex coordination of many trades, and for hundreds of years little significant work was produced. The populace simply lived within the remnants of decaying Roman architecture. After several centuries, governments gradually reasserted order and construction began again, especially for the needs of the most extensive new power in Western Europe—the Catholic Church. From the sixth to the fifteenth centuries, knowledge of the amazing creations of the Romans was regained in part. During the Renaissance the name of the later era of this medieval period would be designated Gothic, implying that it was not classical but of a form created by the barbarians. And "medieval" and "Middle Ages" are pejorative terms indicating a period between the great eras of the classical world and the Renaissance.

THE RENAISSANCE OF ROMAN INFLUENCE

Rome was never forgotten, but its political influence waned and its former glory was reduced to decaying structures in collapse or being used as stone yards for the construction of other less glorious, more utilitarian buildings. Leon Battista Alberti (1404–1472) referred to the remnants of the great Roman culture as "this vast shipwreck."[17] Roman architecture influenced medieval architecture in bits and pieces, but the classical revival began in earnest in the fifteenth century in Florence, largely due to the efforts of one individual: Filippo Brunelleschi (1377–1446). His influence on later

architecture was immense. After abandoning a career as a sculptor, following the well-known competition for the Florence Baptistery doors, Brunelleschi turned his brilliant mind to architecture. To educate himself on his new passion, he traveled to Rome accompanied by his young friend Donatello (1386–1466). His self-education included the study of surviving Roman buildings, especially the Pantheon; details no longer apparent in the ruins were learned from his reading of Vitruvius, as well as from his study of later Byzantine and medieval buildings. Brunelleschi returned proportional order to design along with the details of classical columns and moldings that later architects developed with even closer reference to their classical predecessors. His ornamental treatment of the Pazzi Chapel is an essay in rational organization that became a hallmark of the renewal of classical principles (fig. 1.26).

Vitruvius served as the window into understanding the details of Roman architecture, and his influence was far greater in the fifteenth century than in the first century. His *De Architectura* had been known throughout the Middle Ages, but his influence blossomed with the "discovery" by Poggio Bracciolini (1380–1459) of a particularly fine and complete version of the book at the monastery library of St. Gallen. Creating a personal library became a popular pastime for the wealthy, and sending out humanist scholars to expand their libraries was an essential exercise. Fragments of Latin texts were found and purchased, which fed the growing interest in the land's classical past. New translations of Vitruvius were written and illustrated, further disseminating knowledge of Roman architecture.

Completed in 1452 and published in 1482, Alberti's *De re aedificatoria* (*On the Art of Building in Ten Books*) was the first book of architectural theory since Vitruvius and reproduced many details from Vitruvius including its division into ten books. The first five books draw greatly from Vitruvius, but Alberti devoted most of the remaining books to the subject of beauty. In his new rational approach, he wrote, "Beauty is that reasoned harmony of all the parts within a body, so that nothing may be added, taken away, or altered, but for the worse."[18] This almost mathematically clear concept characterized Renaissance architecture into the first decade of the 1500s.

THE RENAISSANCE PALAZZO AND VILLA

The concept of a pleasure villa was present in both the Roman and Renaissance periods, but times were too unsettled in the Middle Ages to live leisurely within gardens except for temporary visits to the cloisters of monasteries for rest and renewal. Alberti addressed this absence of accommodation for the wealthy in both the urban house—the palazzo—and the more remote residence of the gentleman— the villa, distinct from the rural farm where productive work occurred. He describes in great detail the appropriate location of such buildings and their need to satisfy both use and comfort, and he ends his coverage of residences with comments that influenced the designs of later architects and are appropriate for consideration in current residential planning. In his summary of room design and placement, he wrote:

> Parts that require light until dusk, such as reception halls, passageways, and, in particular, libraries, should face the direction of the sunset at equinox. Anything at risk from moths, mustiness, mold, or rust, such as clothes, books, tools, seed, and any form of food, should be kept in the east or south side of the house. Anywhere an even light is required by painter, writer, or sculptor should lie on the north side. Finally, face all the summer rooms to receive Boreas, all winter ones6to the south; spring and autumn ones toward the sunrise; make the baths and spring dining rooms face the sunset. But if it is impossible to arrange the parts as you might wish, reserve the most comfortable for the summer. To my mind, anyone who is construct-

[1.26] *Filippo Brunelleschi's interior for the Pazzi Chapel (1429–61) at Santa Croce, Florence, surrounds the viewer in an ordered world dominated by rational proportional relationships expressed through a calm palette of white plaster walls divided by decoration in grey pietra serena.*

[1.27] *The Palazzo Davanzati (second half of the fourteenth century), in Florence, exemplifies the transition from the tight, often irregular shape of the medieval tower house to the new ordered concept of the Renaissance palazzo. The irregular plan of the "Room of the Parrots" is evidenced by the ceiling beams. Walls ornamented with frescoes evoke the appearance of textiles, and comfort is provided by the fireplace.*

[1.28 OPPOSITE] *The Renaissance interiors of the Ducal Palace in Urbino characterize the clarity of detail admired by patrons of the fifteenth century. Architect Luciano Laurana (c. 1420–1479) redecorated and expanded the medieval palace, producing for his patron, Federico da Montefeltro, expansive rooms carefully detailed with limited decoration of corbels and chimneypieces, as here in the Room of the Angels.*

ing a building will construct it for summer use, if he has any sense; for it is easy enough to cater to winter: shut all openings, and light the fire; but to combat heat, much is to be done, and not always to great effect. Make your winter living area, therefore, modest in size, modest in height, and with modest openings; conversely, make your entire summer living area in every way spacious and open. Build it so that it will attract the cool breezes but exclude the sun and the winds coming from the sun. For a big room filled with air is like a lot of water in a large dish: it is very slow to warm.[19]

The first palazzo of the Renaissance was designed by Michelozzo di Bartolomeo for the Medici family in Florence. New buildings to display the wealth and refinement of the Pazzi, Strozzi, and Pitti families in Florence, as well as those for the new wealthy in other cities, soon followed the style-setting form of the Palazzo Medici. The designs are orderly in both the planning of their rooms and in the organized appearance of their main facades. By contrast, medieval palazzi might be immensely disorganized in plan, and their facades were proportionally more vertical. In Florence, the Palazzo Davanzati is an excellent surviving example of the medieval palazzi's erratic plan, circulation stair open to the rain and snow, and walls covered with patterned frescoes (fig. 1.27). Overall, the medieval house was a less pleasant arrangement than the comforts enjoyed in the Renaissance—a situation that made the new architecture the envy of the wealthy throughout Europe. Few of the Early Renaissance palazzo interiors of Florence survive intact, but their appearance would likely have been calm white walls with gray stone trim and fireplace mantels with frescoes in some rooms (fig. 1.28).

As it had in the Roman period, perspective again intrigued artists and patrons alike and the rediscovery of the laws that governed it led to its ongoing development throughout the following centuries. Brunelleschi is credited with rediscovering the geometry of perspective that had been known by the Romans, and Alberti recorded this information

in his book *Della Pittura* (*On Painting*). A particularly significant interior of the Early Renaissance survives in Mantua in the ducal palace of the Gonzaga family (figs. 1.29, 30; 6.10). Its Camera degli Sposi (1465–74), or bridal chamber, by Andrea Mantegna is ornamented with frescoes of court life. The ceiling contains an illusionistic oculus with playful putti, a peacock, and court members looking down into the room. The unusual perspective is typical of Mantegna's experiments with dramatic viewpoints. In Urbino, the Studiolo, or small study, of Federico da Montefeltro incorporates a different use of perspective through the finest display of intarsia (scenes in wood inlay) of this era. The small room contained his valu-

able library in casework fronted with illusionistic scenes depicting musical and astronomical instruments, an hourglass, books on shelves, and half-open cabinet doors (fig. 1.31). The upper walls displayed portraits of significant personages. A second studiolo created for Montefeltro's castle in his birthplace of Gubbio is now on display in its entirety in the Metropolitan Museum of Art in New York City.

The designs of villas offered greater variety of arrangement then those of urban palazzi due to unencumbered sites on large estates far from the confinement of city streets. Villa life offered freedom from the social strictures demanded of city life and its responsibilities, and the character of the villa

[1.29] *The north and west walls of Andrea Mantegna's (1431–1506) Camera degli Sposi in the Ducal Palace in Mantua, in walnut oil on plaster, portray changing viewpoints from the meeting scene of the west wall with portraits of Gonzaga and his sons seen at eye level to the lower viewpoint toward seated portraits, above the fireplace, of members of Gonzaga's family, court, and pet dog.*

[1.30] *Mantegna decorated the low ceiling of the Camera degli Sposi with the fresco of a fictive oculus realistically portraying the foreshortened perspective of figures looking into the room from above.*

[1.31] *In the private study of Duke Federico da Montefeltro in the Ducal Palace in Urbino, the intarsia work by Baccio Pontelli, likely from designs by Francesco di Giorgio, Botticelli, and Bramante, masterfully presents through the device of trompe l'oeil paneling the learned interests of the duke in the collection and study of books, music, religion, architecture, and scientific instruments.*

[1.32] *The Loggia of Cupid and Psyche, Villa Farnesina, Rome, served as a stage for performances to entertain the guests of Agostino Chigi. Appropriate to the wealth of the patron, the floor and walls are covered with marble, and the ceiling is frescoed as an imaginative tapestry stretched between an openwork structure covered with rich garlands. The theme of ancient gods and goddesses typifies the Renaissance patron's interest in antiquity.*

[1.33] *The culminating event in the ceiling fresco of the loggia of the Villa Farnesina is titled* The Marriage of Cupid and Psyche *(1518). Raphael Sanzio (1483–1520) portrayed episodes from the fable of Psyche as though drawn upon a tapestry, thus presenting the figural groups without the perspective foreshortening otherwise required for images on a ceiling. Artists from Raphael's workshop employed on this work included Giovanni da Udine, Giulio Romano, Raffaellino del Colle, and Gianfrancesco Penni.*

[1.34] *Baldassare Peruzzi (1481–1536) is credited with the design of the Villa Chigi, later renamed Villa Farnesina. For his finest interior, the second-floor Room of the Perspective Views (1519), Peruzzi employed real marble in the door casings and floors and matched their veining in the faux marble illusion of pilasters and columns; he also extended the patterned flooring into loggias that provide distant landscape views.*

reflected this relaxed attitude. Three villas from the first decades of the sixteenth century indicate the love of antiquity characteristic of the educated wealthy and their desire to integrate art and architecture into their private lives. In the Trastevere section of Rome, the Villa Farnesina, originally Villa Chigi, presents the developing character of the villa form. Although separated from Rome by only the span of the Tiber River, the home of Agostino Chigi, said to be the wealthiest man in Europe, provided privacy for entertainment in his house and its gardens (figs. 1.32, 33). The design represents the efforts of prominent artists and architects then in Rome working for the papacy. The building

itself combines two characters: the street view presents the appearance of a regular two-story palazzo while the private garden side breaks from the expected regular geometry with its U-shape. The original entry into the villa occurred through the central loggia, which is decorated with scenes from Ovid's *Metamorphoses*. The particular interactions between Eros and Psyche are appropriate for the sensual nature of the villa. Baldassare Peruzzi (1481–1536) designed the overall building, and his talents as an artist resulted in the frescoes for the Room of the Perspective Views (fig. 1.34). Here views of Rome are glimpsed through illusionistic loggias that dematerialize the walls and expand

the dimensions of the room. Assisting him in the decoration of other rooms were the artists Raphael, Giulio Romano, Sebastiano del Piombo, and Il Sodoma.

In the following decade, the Villa Madama offered Cardinal Giulio de' Medici, later Pope Clement VII, a place for entertainment and relaxation. Inspired by the written description of the personal villa of the Roman writer Pliny the Younger, Raphael (1483–1520) designed the villa in 1518. After Raphael's premature death, the work was continued by the great artists and architects of the period: Antonio da Sangallo, Peruzzi, and Romano. Work essentially ceased during the Sack of Rome in 1527 and the villa remained only partially complete. In even its partial realization, the magnificent triple-bay domed loggia, decorated with designs inspired by the recently uncovered excavations of Nero's Domus Aurea, is one of the finest interiors in Rome (fig. 1.35). If fully realized, the villa would have included a circular arrival court leading to a semicircular theater inserted into the hill, and formal walled gardens in geometrical patterns cascading down Monte Mario to the Tiber River. The site and building indicate the continuing inspiration provided by memories of Rome and its grandeur.

The third villa is associated with Federico Gonzaga, who invited Giulio Romano (1499–1546) to contribute his talents as artist and architect in the service of the Gonzaga court in Mantua. Romano's greatest contribution to the family involved the expansion of a small structure into the impressive Mannerist composition known as Palazzo Te (fig. 1.36). Although named a palazzo, the structure functioned in all manners as a villa both in provision of entertainment and relaxation and also in its placement within immense gardens. The sequence of public and private rooms surrounds an inner square yard. The exterior design is revered for its introduction of complex rhythms and fanciful details such as its slipped triglyphs that seem to indicate the building has itself slipped into a period of decay (fig. 1.37).

[1.35 OPPOSITE] *Ceiling frescoes of the garden loggia of the Villa Madama reflect the style of Roman art revived by Raphael and his studio after viewing the rediscovered subterranean rooms of Nero's Domus Aurea. Designs with thin arabesques, delicate garlands, panel paintings, and Roman coloration used here and in Raphael's work in the Vatican Loggie inspired similar designs in England in later centuries.*

[1.36] *In Giulio Romano's design for the Palazzo Te, in Mantua, ornamental vocabulary expands through overlapping details, variety of scale, and playful deviations from orthodox usage of classical elements. Accenting the main axis is an arch boldly defined by rusticated voussoirs with a slipped and projecting keystone squeezed between Doric pilasters.*

[1.37] *The northwest wall of the interior courtyard of the Palazzo Te displays the hallmarks of Mannerist design. A recognizable Doric frieze has slipping triglyphs and blank metopes replaced with windows, irregular column spacing, and various levels of rustication—all breaks from orthodox classical language opening up immense new possibilities of expression.*

[1.38] *The Hall of the Horses was the principal entertainment room in the Palazzo Te. On the frescoed walls, an armature of Corinthian pilasters is accented with life-size portraits of Federico II Gonzaga's favorite horses.*

[1.39] *The Chamber of Amor and Psyche (1526–28) received more elaborate decoration than other rooms in the Palazzo Te. The ceiling contains twenty-two episodes from the story of Amor (Cupid) and Psyche, while the walls relate the preparations for a banquet of the gods.*

[1.40] *For the Room of the Giants, Giulio Romano created a continuous fresco seamlessly connecting walls and vaulted ceiling, and, according to Vasari, the original floor of river pebbles continued the scene as well. The effect is unnerving, with Jupiter throwing thunderbolts and caves and columns collapsing at the moment the giants' destructive defeat is captured.*

The interior decorations vary dramatically in theme and artistic scale. The spacious Hall of the Horses is uniquely ornamented with lifelike fresco portraits of favorite stallions from the breeding farm elegantly placed above door architraves (fig. 1.38). The dining room fresco depicts the wedding feast of Cupid and Psyche in a vividly erotic tableau (fig. 1.39). The most memorable of all is the Room of the Giants, created for the visit of Emperor Charles V (fig. 1.40). Decorated with images of the battle between the giants and the Olympian gods, the unnerving scenes of falling rocks and a collapsing world were a facetious presentation by the host to his guest the emperor: although Charles V defeated King Francis I of France and he might have been considered to be the most powerful individual in Europe, his world was subject to collapse within the sphere of the Gonzaga family.

PALLADIO

The spread of villa design throughout Europe and the Americas developed from the unlikely source of the farms landward from the patrician city of Venice. The coincidental reclamation of expansive areas of the marshy Veneto region and the need for elegant homes for the owners of these working farms created the opportunity for an immensely talented stonemason to achieve international renown as the creator of the idealized villa form. Andrea di Pietro della Gondola (1508–1580)—renamed Andrea Palladio, an allusion to Pallas Athene, by his patron Gian Giorgio Trissino—is considered the most imitated architect in the western world. Unlike Raphael or Peruzzi, whose designs were inspired by Roman villas, Palladio created a form dominated by rational geometric and proportional relationships. The buildings were ideal bodies, like the human form, with a central spine and carefully conceived rooms balanced to either side of the central axis. His inspiration developed from his travels to Rome and the study of more far-flung Roman sites along the Adriatic Sea. His integration of the Roman temple facade onto residential structures—a hallmark of entry without the religious association of the original form—became a primary detail in residential design for centuries. Palladio's villas were seasonal homes for their owners, whose principal residence could be found in Venice. The villas are scattered through the countryside surrounding the small town of Vicenza and could never have exerted an influence on future design had Palladio not presented his ideas through the publication of *I quattro libri dell'architectura* (1570).

Palladio's villa designs shared numerous characteristics including axial approach, either a single- or two-story temple facade, bilateral symmetry in plan, and room proportions related three dimensionally (fig. 1.41). His concern for the relationship of each room's width, length, and height was a new contribution to Late Renaissance design. Concern with the association of a room's width and length had been expressed by Alberti a hundred years earlier, but Palladio raised the concept to the entirety of the space that composes a room, and this interest continues to be a hallmark of the work of many of the current classical architects included in this book.

Two villas, Emo and Rotonda, represent the variety Palladio achieved through his design philosophy. Villa Emo (1559–65) was the elegant residence of the Emo family, whose wealth, in part, owed to the verdant acreage surrounding the villa (figs. 1.42, 43). Approached on axis, an impression of great size is created by the arcaded wings that meet at the central four-columned temple facade. The elegant family living spaces reside within the central building mass. All principal rooms follow Palladio's system of ideal proportions, and walls are ornamented with two-dimensional frescoes by Giovanni Battista Zelotti.

[1.41] *The Villa Cornaro, Piombino Dese, Italy (1552–53), exemplifies Palladio's composition of temple-faced balanced villa designs. Due to the popularity of Andrea Palladio's book* I quattro libri dell' architettura *(1570), the temple portico became a popular motif in British and American architecture.*

[1.42] *The bold presence of the Villa Emo, Fanzolo, Italy, upon the flat farmland of the Veneto is enhanced by the biaxial symmetry of arcaded wings flanking the central mass of the main living spaces.*

[1.43] *Palladian villas contain a core room that acts as the heart of villa activity. At the Villa Emo, the main salon is a cubic room of 27 Vicentine feet. This space is among the room shapes Palladio described as most pleasing in his I quattro libri. The walls were decorated with frescoes by Giovanni Battista Zelotti that presented "The Continence of Scipio." This popular theme emphasizing mercy and sexual restraint is based on the Roman writer Valerius Maximus's* Facta et dicta memorabilia *(first century CE).*

[1.44] *This cutaway isometric section of the Villa Rotonda, Vicenza, explains the typically unseen elements in the upper reaches of the design. Palladio's original design included a boldly projecting dome. This shallow dome was an adjustment made by Vincenzo Scamozzi (1548–1616), who finished the building after Palladio's death. The lower dome makes a stronger reference to Roman domes like that of the Pantheon, Rome.*

[1.45] *Palladio's Villa Rotonda inspired the design of numerous buildings from the sixteenth century to the present. The rotunda at Henbury Hall, Cheshire, England (1983), was designed by the British architect Julian Bicknell after a painting by Felix Kelly. This design employs the bolder dome illustrated by Palladio in his* I quattro libri dell'architettura *1570).*

[1.46] *As the Surveyor General of the King's Works, Inigo Jones received numerous commissions including an immense new complex of buildings for Whitehall, London. The only portion constructed by him was the Banqueting House (1619–22). The double-cube room's principal ornamentation is the ceiling, with nine canvases by Peter Paul Rubens that portray attributes of the Stuart kings and significant moments in their history.*

La Rotonda (1556–80) was conceived as a retirement villa and, unlike most of his other villas, it is a solitary cubic form and crowns a hill on the outskirts of Vicenza (fig. 1.44). Palladio was inspired by the Pantheon, so within the Rotonda's cubic shape resides a cylinder topped by a dome. Halls lead from the center to four identical porches fronted by duplicate temple facades. Between the halls, small and large rectilinear rooms are arranged on axes that terminate at windows giving views of the surrounding landscape. Everything is balanced and harmonious within this ideal villa. The iconic form of temple facade and low Roman dome continues to inspire new work based on the subtle beauty of its composition; for example, Julian Bicknell produced Henbury Hall in Britain as his interpretation of these elegant predecessors (fig. 1.45).

After Palladio's death, the villas were first studied by the English architect Inigo Jones (1573–1652), who visited Vicenza on several occasions in the early 1600s. By this time, Palladio was no longer fashionable. His static proportional designs lacked the growing interest in emotional dynamism and bold ornamentation that marked current taste in seventeenth-century Italy. Jones, considered the first English Renaissance architect, saw the beauty in Palladio's villas, palazzos, and churches and drew inspiration from the rigorous simplicity of its classical language. His own great works of the Queen's House in Greenwich (fig. 7.2) and the Banqueting House in London (fig. 1.46) demonstrate the immense potential in the work of Palladio. The lasting influence of Palladio's legacy continued in the eighteenth century through visits by British gentlemen like Lord Burlington and the later translation of his work into English by Nicholas Dubois and Giacomo Leoni in 1721 and by Isaac Ware in 1738 (fig. 1.47). Palladio's writing has remained in print for more than four hundred years with the most recent English translation published in 1998.[20]

THE INFLUENCE
OF ROMAN BAROQUE

In the late sixteenth and seventeenth centuries, Rome became the center of taste, and architects in all countries from Europe to Russia emulated the compositional unity established by the artistic talents brought to Rome to serve the artistic needs of the Vatican. The Roman Baroque was dominated by three great geniuses of design: Gian Lorenzo Bernini, Francesco Borromini, and Pietro da Cortona. Each artistic giant produced their own unique work, but they shared common concepts of the period: high emotionalism, three-dimensionality, exuberant use of materials, and interpretable themes (figs. 1.48, 49, 50). The rationality of earlier Renaissance work was replaced with the operatic drama achieved through colored marbles, illusionistic frescoes that expanded space to infinity, and sculptures that seemed to pulse with life beneath their Carrara marble skin. The boundaries of the realistic world and the illusory world disappeared. Hidden light sources, holes in space with tumbling, playful putti, and extraordinary opulence became the hallmarks of the Roman Baroque.

By the late seventeenth century, France had achieved the position of social arbiter through the reign of the Sun King Louis XIV (1638–1715). The design concepts produced in Rome formed the basis for the French Baroque but were adjusted to fit the heritage and climate of France. Originally a hunting lodge, Versailles was transformed into a setting appropriate for the most powerful throne in Europe. The classical setting employed ideas formulated in the Roman Baroque and took them to new heights of extravagance (fig. 1.51).

Desire for the new Baroque style reached England through the figure of Sir Christopher Wren (1632–1723). He never visited Italy to see actual Roman Baroque architecture but learned of the new elegant style during a visit to Paris in 1665 on his solitary visit abroad. From this inspiration, he

[1.47] *Venetian architect and editor of the first English translation of Palladio's* Four Books of Architecture, *Giacomo Leoni used his knowledge of Palladio in the design of Clandon Park (1720s). Clandon's most spectacular room is Marble Hall, a 40-foot cube with stucco ceiling ornament depicting mythical scenes of Hercules and Omphale by the Venetian artist Giuseppe Artari and two overmantels by the Flemish sculptor John Michael Rysbrack.*

[1.48] *In a side chapel of Santa Maria della Vittoria in Rome, Gian Lorenzo Bernini provides a sensuous view into the ecstatic vision of St. Teresa of Avila as she is pierced by the arrow of heavenly love. The figures of angel and saint are suspended in air before golden rays of sun lighted by a window hidden behind the curving broken pediment above the altar (1647–52).*

[1.49] *Sant'Ivo alla Sapienza (1642–61) is a central-plan church located along the courtyard of the University of Rome. Its architect, Francesco Borromini, employed familial symbols of three successive popes— Urban VIII Barberini, Innocent X Pamphilj, and Alexander VII Chigi—to maintain their patronage. Reflecting the six-sided bee cell, the plan merges at the cornice with the dome creating the complex faceted shape that resolves into a circle. The dome's magnificent plasterwork contains complex manipulations of Chigi symbols including stars, oak wreaths, and flaming triple mountains.*

[1.50] *Pietro da Cortona produced decorations and paintings for the planetary rooms in the Galleria Palatina, located on the second floor of the Palazzo Pitti, in Florence, then occupied by the Medici grand-dukes. The decoration of the Room of Venus (1641–42) includes gilded plaster architectural frames with trompe l'oeil paintings of gods and goddesses opening into spatial infinity. This new interior decoration became the popular style for the residences of European nobility.*

SURVEY OF CLASSICAL INTERIOR DESIGN

[1.51 ABOVE] *For the expansion of the Château de Versailles, Charles Le Brun designed opulent interiors in concert with architect Louis Le Vau and landscape designer André Le Nôtre. A further expansion by François Mansart produced the Salons of War, seen here, and Peace (1678–86) at either end of the Hall of Mirrors. The new style, inspired by the interiors of Pietro da Cortona, incorporated marble panels with gilded bronze carvings and vaulted ceilings with illusionistic paintings. The oval plasterwork bas-relief by Antoine Coysevox presents Louis XIV in a heroic equestrian pose.*

[1.52 OPPOSITE] *Architect C. R. Cockerell created this watercolor capturing the immense contribution of Wren to the architectural character of London. In the misty distance, the great structural achievement of St. Paul's Cathedral dome crowns a composition of fifty-five buildings created by Wren including thirty-three churches. The drawing was exhibited in the Royal Academy in 1838.* A Tribute to Sir Christopher Wren, Charles Robert Cockerell *(1788–1863).* Private Collection, The Bridgeman Art Library

[1.53] *Sir John Vanbrugh designed Castle Howard, Yorkshire (beginning 1701), with assistance from Nicholas Hawksmoor. The immense symmetrical design spreads from the domed central block in a theatrical gesture in keeping with its playwright designer.*

[1.54 OPPOSITE] *Blenheim Palace (1705–22), the greatest achievement of English Baroque style, resulted from the collaboration of Vanbrugh and Hawksmoor. The 67-foot-high Great Hall is the centerpiece of the immense estate house. The stone carvings by Grinling Gibbons celebrate Queen Anne and John Churchill, First Duke of Marlborough. The estate was a gift of the nation for Marlborough's success at the Battle of Blenheim, which is the theme of the Great Hall ceiling painting by Sir James Thornhill (1716).*

developed a new style in England that reflected his more rational scientific bent. His contributions to English architecture were vast, due in part to the devastation wrought upon London by the Great Fire of 1666. Wren was selected to oversee the reconstruction of fifty-three churches, including the Cathedral of St. Paul, that had burned beyond repair. Through this work and other projects for the crown, Wren's office became the training ground for a generation of architects including Nicholas Hawksmoor and Sir John Vanbrugh (figs. 1.52, 53, 54).

Later, during the eighteenth century, Britain caused a new design revolution through the personal experience of travel—not the architects this time, but the patrons themselves, discussed in the following chapter.

CHAPTER TWO

Grand Tour as Influence on Neoclassical Design

CAROL A. HRVOL FLORES

[2.1] Ancient Rome, *1757, Giovanni Panini.* Metropolitan Museum of Art

[2.2] *Sir William Hamilton (1730–1803) with other connoisseurs, meeting of the Society of Dilettanti (engraving), Sir Joshua Reynolds*

[2.3 OPPOSITE] The Campo Vaccino, *before 1751, Piranesi.* British Architectural Library, Royal Institute of British Architects

The Grand Tour, a period of one to two years of travel on the Continent, grew in importance in the early seventeenth century, resulting in citizens from all the nations of Europe converging in Italy to study art and architecture (figs. 2.2, 3). The British were the largest group of travelers and, by the beginning of the eighteenth century, they considered a Grand Tour to be an essential component in the proper education of a gentleman.[1] As a result, thousands of middle- and upper-class men, and a substantial number of women, developed a collective classical consciousness manifest in an appreciation for the art, music, and architecture of Europe. The experiences and knowledge gained on the Grand Tour inspired a cultural revolution in British interiors and a new Golden Age of aesthetic achievement.[2]

Most of the Tourists, derisively called *milordi inglesi* by the Italians, eagerly purchased art, antiques, and books to commemorate their travels, but many pursued such aggressive collecting of relics and fragments that, as early

[2.4 OPPOSITE] Modern Rome, *1757,*
Giovanni Panini. Metropolitan Museum of Art

[2.5 RIGHT] *The Print Room, Uppark*
(before restoration). Engravings of Old Master
paintings, famous architectural sites, and
landscape scenes were mounted on backing
paper and displayed as a collection or miniature
picture gallery. National Trust of Britain

[2.6 BELOW RIGHT] Capriccio *of Roman*
ruins, 1741, Giovanni Paolo Panini. Walker
Art Gallery, Liverpool, UK. English Heritage

as 1730, Italian virtuosi amused themselves by saying that if the amphitheater in Rome were portable, the British would surely carry it off![3] Not all Italians were amused, however; the papacy responded to the Tourists' zeal by acquiring masterpieces of painting and sculpture to protect and preserve Italy's cultural heritage. They expanded existing museums and created a vast new complex in the Vatican to house their enlarged collections.[4] The papacy also influenced the adoption of regulations restricting the excavation and exportation of the country's most precious treasures.[5] These measures did not prevent smuggling of some prized remains and objects of art, however, nor did they prohibit travelers from accumulating legitimate collections of original paintings by Canaletto, Claude Lorrain, the Poussins, and Salvator Rosa.[6]

The fervent desire to collect inspired new works, including the production of copies of busts and antique statuary in bronze and other materials, as well as the commissioning of artists to reproduce antique paintings, the Old Masters, and contemporary works. A substantial industry also grew in engravings, both depictions of existing buildings and Roman ruins as well as the fantastic compositions (*capricci* or *vedute ideate*) where representations of existing ruins were placed in fictitious contexts (figs. 2.1, 4). *Capricci* by Giovanni Paolo Panini (1691–1765) and Giovanni Battista Piranesi (1720–

[2.7] Villa Albani, *c. 1771, Piranesi.*
British Architectural Library, Royal
Institute of British Architects

[2.8 OPPOSITE LEFT] *Sir Harry*
Fetherstonhaugh (1754–1846), painted by
Batoni in 1776. Batoni painted Sir Harry's
parents (Sir Matthew Fetherstonhaugh, 1714–
1774, and Sarah Lethieullier Fetherstonhaugh,
Lady Fetherstonhaugh, d. 1767) two times. In
the first instance, he painted the couple and
their travel companions in 1751, while the
newlyweds were on Grand Tour (1749–51)
selecting and commissioning art and furniture
for the redecoration of Uppark, in West Sussex.
National Trust of Britain

[2.9 OPPOSITE RIGHT] Colonel the Hon.
William Gordon, *Pompeo Batoni, 1766.*
The National Trust for Scotland

1778) were particularly desired and once transported back to the traveler's home would be prominently displayed in rooms and galleries created to exhibit Grand Tour acquisitions (fig. 2.5). One Englishman, Henry Blundell, even commissioned a rotunda based on the Pantheon to house his acquisitions, including a Roman *capricci* by Panini (fig. 2.6).[7]

The Tourists moved throughout Italy taking advantage of changes in climate and local festivals held in Florence, Venice, and Naples, but the center of the Grand Tour experience was residence in Rome. The typical Tourist stayed six

weeks in the city, spending several hours each day with a tutor or guide (*vetturino* or *ciceroni*), who accompanied the visitor and explained the recommended sights. Places considered essential for study included the ancient Roman Forum, the Colosseum, and the Baths of Diocletian, plus St. Peter's Basilica and other Christian churches. Another expected stop was the Villa Albani (1746–50s; fig. 2.7), designed in the style of a Roman country house, and containing the extraordinary collection of art and classical sculpture accrued by Cardinal Alessandro Albani, a respected dealer in antiquities.[8]

In addition to sightseeing and shopping, most Tourists commissioned busts or portraits of themselves from one of the large group of artists resident in Rome.[9] The most privileged commissioned likenesses from Pompeo Batoni (1708–1787), who painted portraits of over two hundred Englishmen between 1740 and 1787, or by the German artist Anton Raphael Mengs (1728–1779). Batoni and Mengs often posed their patrons before architectural monuments to memorialize the subjects' travels and convey an impression of acquired taste (figs. 2.8, 9).

Commissioning likenesses and obtaining art objects constituted the focus of many travelers who found sightseeing and studying boring and preferred to spend their time gambling, drinking, and cultivating social relationships with their countrymen. The depth of learning they acquired was as thin as the canvases used to capture their proud images. Their behavior, ignorance, and extravagance was caricatured in the popular plays of Samuel Foote, the cartoons of Thomas Rowlandson, and the paintings of Thomas Patch, who called these travelers "The Golden Asses."[10]

Upon returning to England, the "Asses" adopted one of two postures. They either became adamant Anglophiles, whose prejudices against anything foreign had been confirmed by the hazards and inconveniences of European travel, or they affected an "undiscriminating preference for all things continental."[11] Although entertaining, these travelers contribute little to understanding the significance of the Grand Tour, unmistakable in those who expanded their knowledge and appreciation of the arts through serious study. Johann Zoffany (1733–1810) depicts this committed group

in a painting entitled *The Tribuna of the Uffizi* (1772–77; fig. 2.10). Zoffany's subjects exhibit the intellectual curiosity and cultivated sensibilities of fine arts connoisseurs. These are the Tourists who embarked on a cultural Odyssey and, upon returning to England, employed the ideas and objects gained during their travels to transform British taste. They became the patrons of the classically inspired art, architecture, and landscapes that form the true legacy of the Grand Tour.

One of the earliest Grand Tourists and the most prominent patron of the arts and architecture during the first half of the eighteenth century was Richard Boyle, the 3rd Earl of Burlington, 4th Earl of Cork, and 4th Baron Clifford of Lanesborough (1694–1753). Burlington inherited wealth, vast landholdings, and positions of high social responsibility in his youth, but had little interest in politics or business. He undertook his first Grand Tour in 1714 to study art, returning to England in 1715, the year Colen Campbell (1676–1729) published *Vitruvius Britannicus*, a set of engravings of country house designs by contemporary architects. Campbell's work introduced Burlington to the study of architecture and "the antique simplicity of Inigo Jones."[12] Jones (1573–1652), "the British Vitruvius," had introduced the ideas of the Italian architect Andrea Palladio (1508–1580) and the classical principles of the Italian Renaissance to Britain during the seventeenth century in masterpieces such as the Queen's House, Greenwich (1616–35), and the Banqueting House, Whitehall, London (1619–22).

Burlington determined to initiate a renaissance of the arts in England and to lead a new Palladian movement, replacing

the extravagance of Baroque architecture with the stylistic purity and structural honesty associated with antique architecture. In 1717, he financed Campbell's second volume of *Vitruvius Britannicus* and commissioned him to remodel Burlington House in London in the new Palladian style. In 1719, Burlington journeyed through Italy studying Palladio's drawings and buildings. He purchased the architect's drawings and enough other art and artifacts to fill 878 pieces of luggage before returning to London later that year.[13] He also brought artists, musicians, and the painter and designer William Kent (c. 1685–1748) with him, hosting them in Burlington House with the composer Handel and the other artists already in residence. Kent remained a member of the household until his death, sharing friendship and an exceptional artistic collaboration with his patron.

Together, Burlington and Kent dominated and transformed British architecture. For their first project, Chiswick House (1725–29; fig. 2.11), they created a pavilion intended for the display of art, the accommodation of an impressive library, and the entertainment of friends, modeled on Palladio's Villa Capra (Villa Rotonda, begun in 1566). Burlington's design followed Palladian proportions, and Kent's decoration incorporated motifs following Inigo Jones, including broken pediments supported by voluptuous brackets over doorways, friezes of masks and garlands on chimneypieces, and heavily coffered or compartmentalized ceilings.[14] The surroundings Kent created established him as one of the originators of the English landscape garden movement, introducing a painterly approach that "improved" the natural qualities of a site to achieve a composition similar to the idealized scenes of the Roman countryside represented in the landscape paintings of Claude Lorrain and Nicholas Poussin. At Chiswick House (c. 1735), Rousham House (c. 1737), and elsewhere, Kent created landscapes of ideas containing literary and visual references familiar to anyone educated in the classics and the aesthetic scholarship of the Grand Tour.

[2.11 OPPOSITE] *The Gallery, looking toward the Octagonal Room, Chiswick House, Lord Burlington, 1727–29.* English Heritage

[2.12] *Marble Hall, Holkham Hall, William Kent, begun in 1734.* By kind permission of the Viscount Coke and the Trustees of the Holkham Estate

Kent, Burlington, and Thomas Coke, later the Earl of Leicester, worked together on the design and decoration of Holkham Hall, Norfolk (begun in 1734), considered to be the greatest country house of the first half of the eighteenth century and Kent's most representative work.[15] Leicester had assembled an important collection of art and Roman antiquities on his Grand Tour and wanted to show these acquisitions to best advantage. The plan follows an unexecuted design by Palladio characterized by a central structure containing staterooms flanked by four semidetached units for guest quarters, a chapel, the kitchen, and a library. The imposing entrance hall (Marble Hall) combined ideas expressed by Vitruvius and Palladio in a rectangular, columned vestibule with the apsidal configurations demonstrated in Palladio's ecclesiastical architecture (fig. 2.12). For embellishment, Kent added a frieze, a coffered cove ceiling, and fluted Ionic columns.

The works of Burlington and Kent exemplify the architect and decorator as archaeologist, an approach that grew in importance throughout the eighteenth century, advancing scholarship on classical design and inspiring architects to repeat original motifs based upon the detailed study of ancient artifacts or measured drawings. Patrons and groups, such as the Society of Dilettanti, a London club of wealthy Englishmen who had traveled to Italy, financed architectural and archaeological studies in Italy, Greece, and the Middle East, and published some of the measured drawings and findings from these productive expeditions.

One of the best-known examples is the Society's support for the research and publication of the work of the British architects James Stuart (1713–1777) (later called James "Athenian" Stuart) and Nicholas Revett (c. 1721–1804).

Stuart and Revett spent the 1740s studying monuments in Rome before they secured the funding to spend four years in Athens documenting ancient Greek buildings and their decoration.[16] When they returned to London in 1755, Stuart established himself as the leading authority on Neoclassical architecture and began creating furniture and interiors based on antique precedents for members of the Society of the Dilettanti and others.[17]

The Dilettanti were particularly interested in Stuart's designs for John Spencer, 1st Earl Spencer (1734–1783), the great-grandson of Sarah Churchill, Duchess of Marlborough, and grandson of the 3rd Earl of Sunderland, whose substantial fortunes he inherited.[18] In December 1755, Spencer married his childhood sweetheart, an unusual circumstance in an era of arranged aristocratic nuptials, and the wealthy, young couple decided to build a London town house for gracious entertaining and for exhibiting the collection of art Spencer had inherited and then augmented with purchases during and after his Grand Tour.[19] In 1756, he commissioned the architect John Vardy, a pupil of William Kent, to construct Spencer House, overlooking Green Park (1756–66). Colonel George Gray, secretary of the Dilettanti Society, supervised the design and may have suggested that the fashionable Stuart design and furnish the State Rooms on the first floor, or *piano nobile*, after Vardy had completed the shell of the house and the ground-floor rooms, including the famous Palm Room.[20]

Stuart's designs (1759–65) in Spencer House introduce and combine Greek elements with Roman and Renaissance motifs, creating a new, eclectic Neolassicism. The scheme of the Painted Room (1759–65), celebrating the Spencers' happy marriage with the theme "The Triumph of Love," is a

good example of Stuart's fully integrated Neoclassical interior work (fig. 2.13). The frieze in the Painted Room was taken from the Erechtheion in Athens, as was the frieze in Lady's Spencer's dressing room. The form and decoration of the Corinthian columns that screen off the apse at the southern end of the room and the pilasters on the north are based upon the portico of the Temple of Antoninus and Faustina in Rome (begun 141 CE), while the mirror frames and door surrounds are modeled on the fluted frieze in the antique colonnade of the Incantada at Salonica (Thessaloniki) in Greece, later illustrated in Stuart and Revett's *Antiquities of Athens*.[21] Throughout his designs for Spencer House, Stuart sources both Roman and Greek motifs. The chimneypiece of the Painted Room is flanked by two female figures known as terms and continues the marriage theme with a frieze based on the *Aldobrandini Wedding*, a painting excavated in Rome in 1605 and displayed in the Vatican Museum.[22] The plasterwork in the apse incorporates motifs of the Greek key, anthemion, and arabesques. Stuart again incorporated the theme of marriage with his design of a circular grisaille panel depicting a wedding scene derived from a marble relief Stuart found on the Acropolis and painted panels covered in the type of ancient Roman grotesques or arabesques reintroduced in the Renaissance by Raphael, Vasari, and others. The arabesques in the Painted Room copy Raphael's ornament in the Loggie of the Vatican (1515–19).[23]

Stuart also designed classically inspired furniture for the Painted Room. The noted architectural historian David Watkin attributes the sofa design with lion motif to the architect's adaptation of Roman ceremonial furniture carved in marble to domestic seating fashioned in wood. Watkin observes that this modification contributes to the monumental character of the pieces.[24]

The decoration of the Great Room (1764), designed for the display of art and as the setting for receptions and balls, also combined Roman and Greek references (fig. 2.14). The motifs of the friezes, picture frames, and moldings exemplify Greek precedents, while the coved, coffered ceiling imitates Roman form and ornament. The classical theme was accentuated in the ceiling design with bronze plaster medallions depicting Bacchus, Apollo, Venus, and the Three Graces, representing conviviality, the arts, and love and beauty, respectively.[25]

The desire to display paintings and other objects acquired on a Grand Tour produced dramatic changes in British interiors. Affluent patrons commissioned furniture and rooms to exhibit important collections of art, books, and antiquities (figs. 2.15, 16).[26] Tourists with smaller collections and lesser fortunes hung artwork in wood and gilt frames on painted or fabric-covered walls. Great care was taken in the precise arrangement of the images, resulting in balanced, symmetrical compositions. Copies of important paintings were hung alongside original works of art, since copies of great works were believed to be more important than originals by lesser artists.

The publications of Robert Wood, Stuart and Revett, and others, plus the discoveries at Herculaneum and Pompeii in the middle of the eighteenth century, prompted even greater numbers of travelers to Italy to view the excavations.[27] This wave included the young Scottish architect Robert Adam (1728–1792), who used the knowledge and objects acquired on his Grand Tour to introduce a new spirit and style of invention in decoration that dominated British design for over three decades.

Adam, the second son of the celebrated Scottish architect William Adam (1689–1748), joined his father as an apprentice-assistant in 1746 and embarked on a four-year Grand Tour in 1754.[28] The ambitious younger Adam spent his time in Europe in serious study and directed travel. He hired the respected French artist and architect Charles-Louis Clérisseau (1721–1820) to act as his tutor and guide. Clérisseau taught the young Scot the comprehensive plan-

ning and precise handling of details characteristic in French eighteenth-century architecture and instructed him in drawing, history, and archaeology. The pair traveled throughout Italy and present-day Croatia studying architecture and ruins and accumulating the collection of fragments, antiques, and drawings that formed the resource for Adam's publications and designs. When they returned to Rome, Clérisseau supervised the staff of draughtsmen Adam hired to prepare the measured drawings for the *Ruins of the Palace of the Emperor Diocletian, at Spalatro, in Dalmatia* (1764).

Adam's most important relationship was the friendship he established with the well-published antiquarian, architect, and etcher Giovanni Battista Piranesi. Piranesi's dramatic depictions of real and imaginary constructions inspired a new intellectual and artistic freedom in the work of Adam. This spirit of invention set Piranesi and Adam apart from

their contemporaries as well as the masters of the Renaissance. While Renaissance architects had looked to ancient Rome to discover design principles, Piranesi and Adam observed that the ancients hadn't followed prescribed rules but combined motifs and varied proportions as they wished. This realization motivated Adam to modify elements from the past and recombine them in an innovative, Romantic Neoclassicism.

His interior renovations continued to rely on classical precedents and motifs, but, unlike his predecessors, he changed the scale, character, and materials of his sources to produce picturesque compositions where every object and detail was to his design or selection and each element contributed to the decorative effect of the whole. Other characteristics of his style include the abstraction of antique motifs into delicate ornament, the introduction of

[2.15] The Townley Marbles in
the Entrance Hall of 7 Park Street,
Westminster, *1794, William Chambers
(a draftsman, not the architect).*
©The Trustees of the British Museum

lively color schemes accented with stucco or gilding, and, often, the repetition of ceiling patterns in different materials on floors to unify a room (fig. 2.17). His approach evolved from bold, monumental arrangements in the early schemes to refined abstractions in the later commissions. For example, in ceiling design, the heavy coffers and compartments seen in the saloon in Kedleston Hall (1761–62) and the anteroom and entrance hall in Syon House (1761–65) become the lacey patterns evident in the Top Hall, Nostell Priory (1773–75) and the music room at Harewood House (1765–71). He achieved interest and diversity in his ceiling designs by incorporating different shapes, including barrel vaults, coves, and domes, as well as varying the type of decoration from all-over repetitive patterns, to tripartite schemes and arrangements emphasizing a central motif in paint or plaster.

His wall decorations were equally diverse. The pronounced architectural character of the early work, realized through the addition of large columns, half-columns, alcoves and statuary, changed to flat, two-dimensional arrangements incorporating pilasters, plaques, panels, and medallions in ornamental interpretations of the orders. An excellent example of his originality is evident in the decoration of the Etruscan Dressing Room at Osterley Park (1775–76), where he designed ornament based upon the colors and motifs discovered at Pompeii (fig. 2.18). Adam's ideas and techniques were widely adopted by other architects and craftsmen in the 1760s, '70s, and '80s, particularly the potter Josiah Wedgwood (1730–1795) and the cabinetmaker Thomas Chippendale (1718–1779), but by the 1780s and 1790s many designers and patrons began to think that his ornament had become too filigreed and fanciful, and his influence began to wane.

At the end of the eighteenth century, an admirer of Robert Adam, the architect John Soane (1753–1837), developed another distinctive Picturesque interpretation of

[2.16] Charles Townley's Library at 7 Park Street, Westminster, *1781–83, Johann Zoffany. The architectural elements in the painting are correct, but the statues depicted form a picturesque record of antique statues purchased by Townley, though not all were displayed in this room.* Townley Town Hall Art Gallery and Museums, Burnley Borough Council

[2.17] *Library of Kenwood, Robert Adam, 1767–69.* English Heritage

[2.18 OPPOSITE] *Etruscan Room, Osterley Park, Robert Adam, 1775–76*

[2.19 FOLLOWING PAGES] The Plan and Interior of the Ground Floor of a Town House, *1822, Sir John Soane's Museum, London. The interiors in No. 13 Lincoln's Inn Fields, London, by Sir John Soane remain much the same as depicted in this watercolor. The rooms shown include the Monument Court, study, breakfast parlor, library, and dining room.* John Soane Museum, London

classical architecture. His town house, at No. 13 Lincoln's Inn Fields, London (1792), is the best extant example of his unique style, incorporating shallow domes and hidden sources of light and mirrored reflections (*lumiere mysterieuse*) to enhance the art and architectural fragments he collected during his travels and study abroad (fig. 2.19).

In 1796, Napoleon Bonaparte's army occupied Italy, complicating travel and interrupting the steady flow of Grand Tourists to Rome until 1815, when a "renewed phase of enthusiasm for things Roman" occurred.[29] In the meantime, travelers interested in art, archaeology, and architecture had ventured into Egypt, the Middle East, and Spain. These travels continued, sparking lively debates in the nineteenth century over the color and decoration of ancient buildings and generating an enthusiasm for the exotic. Steamships, railroads, and the building of hotels throughout Europe replaced the arduous adventures and hazardous uncertainties of the earlier Grand Tour excursions with the safe and comfortable tours of the Continent arranged by the pioneer of the travel industry, Thomas Cook.[30]

Today, tourists and designers still pursue the cultural legacy and education of the Grand Tour, visiting ancient sites, plus museums and grand houses filled with collections of objects preserved and produced to forge associations with the styles and ideas of earlier eras. As a result, some of these travelers become the patrons of new buildings and interiors inspired by the works of the past. Many of the designers, particularly those included in this book, go on to produce schemes in the tradition of Kent, Stuart, Adam, and Soane. Like their predecessors, they combine historic motifs and techniques with new materials and technology and follow principles of proportion and design identified and defined during the Renaissance. This dedication to the pursuit of classical ideals and an understanding of the aesthetic spirit of the past is the true and continuing legacy of the Grand Tour.

THE·PLAN·AND·INTERIOR·
·OF·THE·
GROVND·FLOOR·
·OF·A·
TOWN·HOVSE·

MARCH·MDCCCXLII

CHAPTER THREE

Classical Revival in the Nineteenth and Twentieth Centuries

ELIZABETH MEREDITH DOWLING

[3.1] *In the Main Reading Room of the Library of Congress in Washington, D.C., 10-foot-high statues above the eight marble columns indicate the immense size of the space designed under the supervision of Edward Pearce Casey.* Courtesy Carol M. Highsmith Archive, Library of Congress, Prints and Photographs Division

[3.2] *Coleshill House (c. 1658–62; destroyed by fire 1952) was designed by the English gentleman-architect Sir Roger Pratt for his cousin. Elements popularized in American Georgian houses include a double-pile design, raising the house on a high basement, symmetrical facades without applied columns, high roof and chimneys, and multiple dormer windows.*

[3.3 OPPOSITE] *The grand staircase at Coleshill House framed the axial entrance to the main saloon. Finished with a finely detailed plaster ceiling, the house exhibits the influence of Inigo Jones.*

AMERICA'S CLASSICAL HERITAGE

As American architecture grew from its infancy in the eighteenth century to maturity in the nineteenth century, architects and patrons depended on sources similar to those of their British counterparts; however, the firsthand knowledge gained through the experience of the Grand Tour was not one of the primary means of engaging classical architecture until late in the nineteenth century. The waters of the Atlantic and the Mediterranean separated Americans from the antique architecture of Rome and Athens, and knowledge came secondhand through books. These books, created through the patronage of British enthusiasts, provided Americans with knowledge to create their fledgling public and private buildings. Most eighteenth-century American architecture sought to replicate as closely as possible the current stylistic trends in the English homeland. American Georgian architecture reflected in much reduced versions the manor houses of the British elite. Built in Oxfordshire during the mid-seventeenth century and destroyed by fire in 1952, Coleshill House, (figs. 3.2, 3), with its symmetrical nine-bay design, hip roof with dormers, and centered entry was the characteristic image employed in the designs of eighteenth-century Virginia Colonial plantation houses like Westover and Carter's Grove (figs. 3.4, 5). The entry stair at

[3.4] *One of the earliest grand mansions in Virginia, Westover Plantation (c. 1730) in Charles City County, faces the James River, which made for easier access to Richmond and Williamsburg. The balanced composition of the main house with its centered entry, hip roof, and dormer windows forms the classic composition of a Georgian house.*

[3.5] *The rectangular entry hall of Carter's Grove (1751) opens through a broad segmental arch to an exquisitely detailed stair. The heart pine paneling, Ionic pilasters on pedestals, and classical cornice are considered by many experts to be the finest Georgian woodwork in Virginia.*

Coleshill House may have influenced the similar double winding stair at Drayton Hall near Charleston, South Carolina, the finest extant example of Georgian Palladian architecture in America (fig. 3.6).

With American independence from England, an accompanying search for more acceptable nationalistic inspiration presented the Neoclassical designs of our French allies as more desirable than those of the English. Thomas Jefferson returned from his position as ambassador to France with knowledge of both Roman architecture and modern French design. He employed both sources in his own Monticello and the University of Virginia campus (figs. 3.7, 8). Detailed information on Roman architecture was presented in Robert Adam's *Ruins of the Palace of the Emperor Diocletian at Spalatro* (1764) and Robert Wood's two books *The Ruins of Palmyra* (1753) and *The Ruins of Balbec* (1757). A plate depicting the Temple of the Sun in Palmyra had served as the inspiration for the East Portico of the United States Capitol designed by Benjamin Latrobe.

Latrobe (1764–1820), and his pupils Robert Mills (1781–1855) and William Strickland (1788–1854), produced sophisticated public buildings often based on Greek precedent rather than Roman. Knowledge of both styles was readily accessible through numerous volumes of carefully measured and drawn plates. James Stuart and Nicholas Revett produced *The Antiquities of Athens and Other Monuments of Greece* as a four-volume set of measured drawings, with the first volume published in 1762.

GREEK REVIVAL IN AMERICA AND EUROPE

The Greek Revival was an international phenomenon appreciated for its sobriety, formality, and restraint. Its associations with Athenian democracy made it an especially appropriate style for government and commercial buildings in America.

[3.6] *Drayton Hall (1738–42) is the oldest surviving example of Georgian Palladian architecture in America. The fine brick house retains its original paneling and one of its original hand-carved plaster ceilings. Drayton Hall stair hall.* Courtesy Drayton Hall, a National Trust for Historic Preservation historic site. Photography by Tony Sweet

[3.7] *The dining room of Monticello (1769–84; 1796–1809) was recently restored to its first coloration of chrome yellow. Jefferson's scientific bent is apparent in his use of double layers of window sash to insulate the room. The Doric order detailing of the elliptical arch opens to the Tea Room.* Thomas Jefferson Foundation at Monticello, photograph by Philip Beaurline

[3.8 OPPOSITE] *The parlor of Monticello is the largest room in the house and was used for social activities. The shape is square with a hexagonal projection opening to the west portico. Jefferson's source for the architectural detailing was the Temple of Jupiter Tonans as illustrated in his copy of Antoine Desgodetz's,* Les edifices antiques de Rome *(1682). The color of the room is unpainted plaster with a parquet floor of cherry and beech designed by Jefferson.* Thomas Jefferson Foundation at Monticello, photograph by Carol Highsmith

CLASSICAL REVIVAL

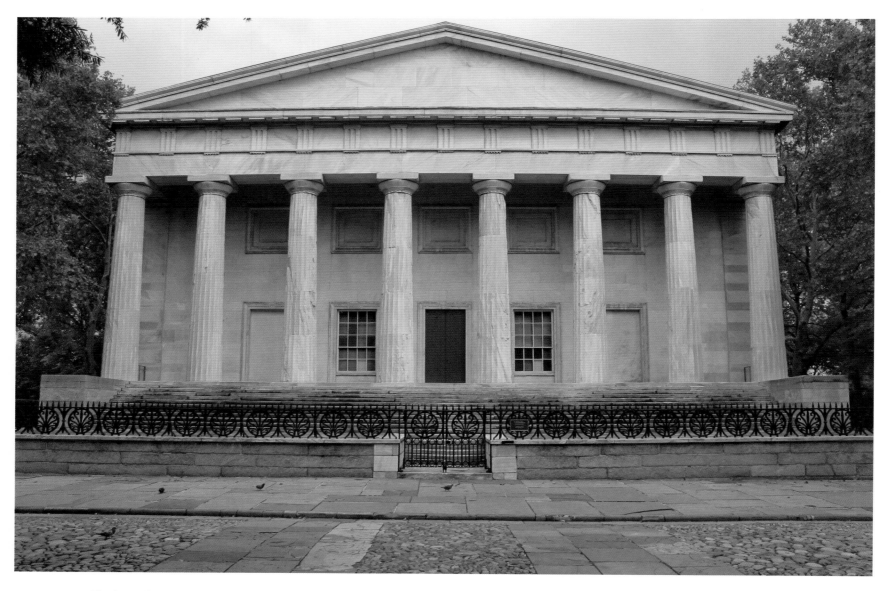

[3.9] *The Second Bank of the United States (1819–24), Philadelphia, designed by William Strickland is a National Historic Landmark. Its status as one of the nation's finest examples of the Greek Revival style is due in large measure to the Hellenic preferences of Nicholas Biddle (1786–1844), the first president of the Second Bank of the United States.*

[3.10] *The Merchant's Exchange Building (1832–34) was designed by William Strickland in America's first national style—the Greek Revival. This office building became the commercial center of Philadelphia, and its dramatic site is marked by the cupola referencing the Choragic Monument of Lysicrates (334 BCE).*

[3.11] *The Choragic Monument of Lysicrates (334 BCE) commemorates a choral victory at the Great Dionysia, an ancient dramatic festival held in Athens. Its six Corinthian columns are the oldest surviving examples of that order. The small structure became well known to the Western world through this engraving published by Stuart and Revett in* The Antiquities of Athens *(1762).*

[3.12] *Numerous capitols in America were designed in the Greek Revival style due to its visual evocation of Athenian democracy. The Tennessee State Capitol (1845–59), designed by William Strickland, attests to the impressive grandeur of America's first national style.*

Examples using Greek precedent include William Strickland's Second Bank of the United States (1819–24) and the Merchant's Exchange Building (1832–34) in Philadelphia (figs. 3.9, 10). For the bank, Strickland employed an eight-columned temple facade based on the Parthenon (447–432 BCE). For the Merchant's Exchange, he more freely employed classical details to fit a circular portico into the urban site. He finished the building with a second curving form—a cupola inspired by the Choragic Monument of Lysicrates (334 BCE) illustrated in James Stuart's *Antiquities of Athens* (fig. 3.11).

Government buildings in the new style include the Tennessee and Illinois State Capitols. For the Tennessee State Capitol (1845–59), Strickland created a monumental building at the highest point in Nashville. The body of the building references an Ionic temple placed above a rusticated base. He placed Ionic porticoes on all four sides and employed the Choragic Monument form to add dramatic height to the crowning cupola (fig. 3.12). In Illinois, John F. Rague designed the State Capitol (1837–40) using local amber-toned stone and the severe Doric order (fig. 3.13). This building served as the backdrop for Abraham Lincoln's famous speech of 1858, known afterward as "The House Divided Speech."

The Greek Revival also served as a popular residential style and could be found throughout the United States during its height from 1820 to the Civil War. The simple elegant classical details could be easily rendered in wood, making it a good economical and aesthetic choice. As Talbot Hamlin

[3.13] *The Old State Capitol in Springfield, Illinois, was designed in the Greek Revival style by John Francis Rague (1799–1877). The somber Greek Doric portico served as the backdrop for the announcement of the presidential candidacies of Abraham Lincoln in 1858 and Barack Obama in 2007.* Courtesy of Illinois Historic Preservation Agency

explained in *Greek Revival Architecture in America* (1944), the Greek Revival appropriately expressed an aesthetic blossoming in America and an educational system that emphasized freethinking, poetry, and an accompanying study of Latin for which Greek and Roman architecture were seen as perfectly acceptable backdrops. In describing this important aesthetic era of American history, Hamlin wrote:

> It was as if man in America, around 1820, had rediscovered his five senses; had suddenly, like one breaking through from the forest to sun-drenched, sea-bordered downs, all at once become conscious of bright sun and distance and freedom; had suddenly discovered that it was better to see and hear beautiful things than ugly ones; had, in a word, waked up from a nightmare. At once the fine arts achieved a position they

had not held before. Education was based on poetry rather than theology, and was an education of the physical senses as well as one based on a sense of duty.[1]

The Greek forms served equally well to project an image of bold grandeur in plantation homes in Louisiana or Mississippi, estates in Pennsylvania, or modest elegance in urban houses in New York, Ohio, or Vermont (figs. 3.14–17). Churches and courthouses in rural towns and large cities equally employed this popular style. This architectural form flourished during an era preceding the burgeoning industrialization of America and the creation of a new financial aristocracy who would choose to renew the spirit of the Grand Tour and demand that their architects produce buildings of

[3.14] *Dunleith (c. 1855) in Natchez is the only extant example of a plantation house in Mississippi fully surrounded by a colonnade. Its significance as a National Historic Landmark is due in part to the survival of its twenty-six Tuscan columns and ornamental iron details.*

[3.15] *In 1806, Benjamin Latrobe designed Andalusia, in Philadelphia, in the English Regency style. Later, when the house served as the residence of Nicholas Biddle, Thomas Ustick Walter expanded it, including this Doric portico (1834–36) with its details patterned after the Temple of Hephaestus located in the Agora, in Athens, Greece (449–415 BCE).* Courtesy The Andalusia Foundation, photograph by Katharine H. Norris

CLASSICAL REVIVAL

[3.16] *The Yellow Parlor in Andalusia, designed by Thomas Ustick Walter, retains its original Greek Revival detailing and is a National Historic Landmark.*
Courtesy The Andalusia Foundation, photograph by Connie S. Griffith Houchins

[3.17] *The Samuel Wadsworth Russell House (1827–29) in Middletown, Connecticut, was designed by the influential American architect Ithiel Town (1784–1844). Town employed not only elegant Corinthian columns for the pedimented facade, but introduced a new open plan that helped popularize the Greek Revival style.*

[3.18] *Holmwood House (1857–58), located in suburban Glasgow, Scotland, is considered the finest residential design of the important Scottish architect Alexander "Greek" Thomson. In the dining room's polychromatic decoration, the frieze was based on drawings by John Flaxman illustrating Homer's Iliad. The palmette, or anthemion motif, appears on the interior and exterior. In the dining room, the palmette visually connects the frieze with imaginative details on pilaster capitals and doors. The house is owned by the National Trust for Scotland.*

[3.19] *As court architect for King Ludwig of Bavaria, Leo von Klenze (1784–1864) designed numerous buildings in the Greek Revival style. The exterior design of Walhalla is based on the Parthenon in Athens with details altered to reflect German history. The main hall is a single skylit space with a wall display of busts of great figures from German history commissioned by King Ludwig.*

[3.20 OPPOSITE] *The Academy of Athens (1859) was designed by the Danish architect Theophil Hansen (1813–1891) as one of a trilogy of buildings including the University of Athens and the National Library. The Neoclassical design connects modern Greece with its classical heritage, embodied in the Parthenon. The Public Meeting Hall is decorated with an immense mural 150 feet in length by the Austrian artist Christian Griepenkerl. Designed by Hansen, the hall's theme portrays the myths of Prometheus and his gift of fire to humans.* Courtesy The Academy of Athens

the scale and pretension they saw in Europe. For a few decades, the Greek Revival had provided a shared aesthetic and a general uniformity in American architecture. This cohesiveness was replaced by the growing interest in numerous styles of architecture as they became known to architects and patrons alike through travel and books.

In Europe, the Greek Revival developed as one facet of Neoclassical architecture. Its popularity varied between nations. France had little interest in the style, while Germany, Sweden, Scotland, Finland, and Russia showed greater interest (figs. 3.18, 19). Examples of Greek Revival could also be found in the newly independent nation of Greece as demonstrated by the work of the Danish architect Theophil Hansen (1813–1891). After training under Karl Friedrich Schinkel, Hansen moved to Athens during a period of significant construction. During his nine-year residence in the city he designed three public works in the Greek Revival style: the National Observatory of Athens, the Academy of Athens (fig. 3.20), and the National Library of Greece. Upon his return to Vienna, he designed the Austrian Parliament Building (1874–83) with politically appropriate references to Greek democracy (fig. 3.21).

AMERICAN RENAISSANCE

By the last decades of the nineteenth century, American architecture changed dramatically through the increased sophistication both of its architects and its patrons. Until 1846, the year Richard Morris Hunt became the first American to enroll at the Ecole des Beaux-Arts in Paris, American training for its architects was through apprenticeship with an established architect. The established architect either immigrated to America with formal training from his home country or informal training through a similar apprenticeship system. Formal European training of architects began in 1671 with the founding in Paris of an Academy of Architecture and its accompanying school, which by 1819

would be known as the Ecole des Beaux-Arts. In *The Beaux-Arts Tradition in French Architecture*, Donald Drew Egbert commented, "From the beginning, the Académie Royale d'Architecture's dominant conception of good architecture was that it exemplified a beauty of form based on fixed principles of taste. These principles were universally accepted by the foremost among those best qualified to judge their merit, and these principles were also teachable."[2] Although instructors demanded no particular style, antiquity and the Italian Renaissance were the foundations of Ecole principles. Clarity of plans, with well-proportioned rooms aligned axially, was found in the study of Roman architecture, the illustrations of Palladio, and the work of other masters of the Renaissance. This system of education

[3.24] *Among the many significant public buildings designed by the firm of John Merven Carrère 1858–1911) and Thomas Hastings (1860–1929), the New York Public Library 1897–1911), with its Astor Library, is one of the finest Beaux-Arts designs in America.*

[3.25 OPPOSITE LEFT] *Arthur Brown, Jr. (1874–1957), designed both the San Francisco City Hall and the adjacent War Memorial Opera House (1927–32). The impressively somber lobby of the opera house employs Roman Doric columns supporting a vault ornamented with rosettes within octagonal coffers.*

[3.26 OPPOSITE RIGHT] *The Neptune Pool is one of the many architectural elements added by architect Julia Morgan (1872–1957) to her design for Hearst Castle, which she worked on from 1919 to 1947. One among numerous projects created by Morgan for William Randolph Hearst, the castle demonstrates the extent of her abilities and it has been designated a National Historic Landmark in recognition of its design excellence.*

evolved over time, but it consistently included lectures on history and theory and the judging of design problems studied independently under the tutelage of an architect selected as a mentor by the student. Typically, some architects worked with a number of students in an atelier, or external studio. The Ecole controlled the design work of students by writing the programs for design problems and judging the results.[3] Other European countries initiated their own forms of architectural education in the eighteenth and nineteenth centuries. Formal education for Americans dates to the establishment of a program in 1865 at Boston Tech, later renamed Massachusetts Institute of Technology. Created by William Ware, this program was based on the methods he learned as an apprentice in the firm of Richard

Morris Hunt, who, in turn, was passing on methods he had learned in Paris. By 1900, ten American universities offered degrees in architecture.[4]

In the last decades of the nineteenth century, students who enrolled in a university that had not yet developed an architecture curriculum often pursued a degree comparable to civil engineering. Since college education was a rarity and often only available to those financially able, a growing number of young men and, rarely, women spent some years in Paris at the Ecole. This additional training provided America with exceptionally sophisticated professional designers who created landmarks of civic and private architecture. Among this exceptional group are Charles F. McKim, Edward Pearce Casey, John Carrère, Thomas

Hastings, Arthur Brown, Jr., John Russell Pope, Julia Morgan, and Whitney Warren.[5] Each of these individuals created exceptional buildings based upon the study of classical design (figs. 3.22–26).

In the first decades of the twentieth century, classical design continued to be taught in the traditional manner in American universities. Students learned to draw the details of Greek and Roman architecture; they were thoroughly schooled in the history of architecture beginning with the roots of monumental architecture created by the Egyptians and continuing to the present day; they took art classes that helped hone their skills in watercolor renderings and taught them to appreciate the proportions of humanistic classical elements by drawing live nude models. By the late 1920s, the details of what would come to be known as Art Deco

became commonplace in design solutions. This stylistic name derived from the 1925 Paris exhibit titled *Exposition des arts décoratifs et industriels moderne*. (Much to the embarrassment of American designers, President Herbert Hoover refused to send an American exhibit to this international exposition.) The popular motifs of electricity, movement, and stylized plant forms along with exotic woods and the new material of aluminum became the hallmarks of the frenetic 1920s design expression (figs. 3.27, 28). Also entering the vocabulary of American designers was the severe industrialized aesthetic promoted by the newly formed Bauhaus, the modern craft-based school in Dessau that operated from 1919 to 1933.

The first challenge to the Beaux-Arts-inspired method of design came in the 1930s, when many professors from the

[3.27] *The U.S. Customs House in Philadelphia (1932–34) is one of the many fine public buildings that was funded through the Works Progress Administration. The fine Art Deco interior designed by architects Ritter & Shay includes murals by artist George Harding.* Courtesy Carol M. Highsmith Archive, Library of Congress, Prints and Photographs Division

[3.28 OPPOSITE] *The two-story rotunda is capped with a spiraling coffer motif filled with gold-leaf shells. Above the eight fluted marble columns, the frieze includes eight mural panels by George Harding depicting the winds using symbols from Greek mythology.* Courtesy Carol M. Highsmith Archive, Library of Congress, Prints and Photographs Division

CLASSICAL REVIVAL

105

[3.29] *John Russell Pope (1874–1937) designed the National Gallery of Art (1937–41), Washington, D.C., with a somber classical temple facade marking the entrance from the National Mall. Behind the temple facade, a coffered dome is expressed on the interior with a rotunda rising above sixteen dark marble columns of the Ionic order.*

[3.30 OPPOSITE] *Although modernist proponents decried Cass Gilbert's design for the Supreme Court Building (1932–35), the architect felt the classical design more appropriately represented a permanent rather than a transitory image and was thus appropriate for the deliberations of the nation's highest court.* Courtesy Franz Jantzen, Collection of the Supreme Court of the United States

Bauhaus immigrated to America to escape persecution in Nazi Germany. Some found positions in architecture schools, where they taught the Bauhaus aesthetic of free-flowing space, large expanses of windows, flat roofs, no applied ornamentation, and use of nontraditional materials. Humanist concerns for beauty, scale, and symbolic expression were replaced with the new formulation that emphasized innovation and technological appearance. The teaching of architectural history was even forbidden, out of an overwhelming desire to make a break with the past. By 1950, most American academic programs had abandoned the teaching of the architectural orders and the Beaux-Arts principles of composition. All that remained of the former system was a use of French terminology and the studio system of design instruction.

Introduction of the modern aesthetic coincided with the economic collapse of the Great Depression in the 1930s. Little was built during this period, and the prospect of economical design offered by the simplified forms of modern architecture appealed to cash-strapped public and private clients. The buildings thus created may not have been built to last, but they were serviceable and affordable. Proponents of this new "modern" style aggressively attacked the traditions of classicism as being out of step with modern life. Unseemly assaults of architect upon architect sometimes took place in the public forum of professional journals. Such buildings in Washington, D.C., as John Russell Pope's National Gallery (1937–41) and Jefferson Memorial (1939–43), and Cass Gilbert's Supreme Court Building (1932–35) were subject to vituperative attacks by modernists who thought publicly funded work should convey current design trends rather than the timeless appearance of classicism (figs. 3.29, 30).

Following the end of World War II, when construction once again picked up, the new aesthetic of European modernism had continuing appeal as a fresh, clean image for a

society remaking itself. Almost no public buildings and only a small percentage of residential work were designed in traditional and classical forms. Glass office buildings, libraries, and city halls replaced their elegant classical and Art Deco predecessors, while the ranch-style house filled the growing suburbs. By the 1950s, the Beaux-Arts-trained architects still in practice were reaching retirement age, and the new generation of modern designers lacked their knowledge of classical design. The craftsmen who created the plaster moldings, stonework, woodcarvings, and decorative ironwork were no longer needed for the creation of unornamented buildings. Without newly trained classical architects, and with the supporting system of trades also disappearing, the possibility of entirely losing the classical tradition became a reality. What the Depression of the 1930s and modern design had not done to end a 2,500-year-old tradition, age and lack of training was accomplishing.

CHAPTER FOUR

Re-creating the Past

ELIZABETH MEREDITH DOWLING

[4.1] *Although the original St. Peter's Basilica no longer exists, the various incarnations of the Basilica of San Clemente, Rome, present the complex story of early Christian church architecture. Beneath the current basilica dating from c. 1100 are the restored remains of a fourth-century church built on the remains of a Roman house and a cult temple of Mithras. The current nave uses unmatched antique columns, also known as spolia, taken from earlier Roman buildings.*

[4.2] *The Cancelleria (1483–1517), Rome, was originally the home of Cardinal Raffaele Riario (1461–1521), a relative of popes Sixtus IV and Julius II, who is credited with inviting Michelangelo to Rome. Riario's enormous palace was constructed with building materials scavenged from many antique buildings including the Colosseum and the Theater of Pompey.*

[4.3 OPPOSITE] *The Theater of Pompey (c. 55 BCE) was the first permanent theater in Rome created of stone and it became the model for all later theaters. In addition to the theater seating and stage, the complex included gardens, fountains, and temples. Columns of Egyptian granite were taken from the theater to build the Basilica of San Lorenzo in Damaso (fourth century CE) and, in turn, were used for the inner courtyard of the palace of Cardinal Riario.*

The 2,500-year-old tradition of classical architecture came close to being extinguished in the mid-twentieth century due to an overwhelming presence of modernist theory in architecture schools throughout the world. The survival of the tradition can be attributed to several factors, including clients who did not find the modernist aesthetic appealing, the development of the preservation movement, which kept craft traditions alive, individual designers whose fascination with classicism caused them to independently seek the knowledge of an extremely complex form of design, and, more recently, the reintroduction of formal training in classical architecture. Without each of these—clients, preservation projects, and independently minded designers—the extensive knowledge and skill required to create classical buildings would have become extinct.

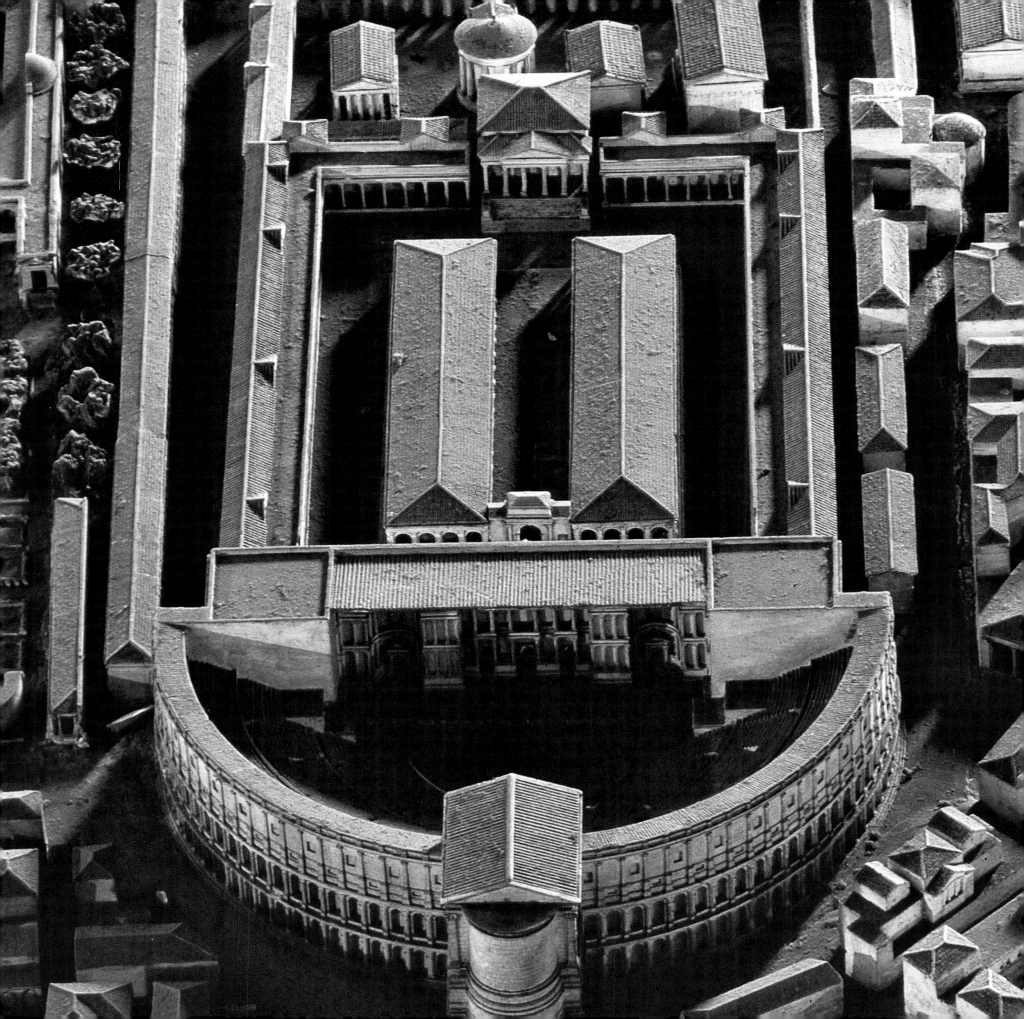

As indicated in previous chapters, later cultures revered the classical architecture of Greece and Rome. For example, Renaissance architects based their theories of design on the understanding of Roman architecture gained from reading Vitruvius and from the study of surviving buildings, but their attitude about preserving the buildings they admired differed greatly from current thoughts about the treatment of monumental buildings of the past. From the sixth century onward, the surviving remains of preexisting structures in the city of Rome were used as a vast stone quarry providing building materials for new construction. During the Middle Ages, the Colosseum (see fig. 2.9) served as a ready source for the lime burners who demolished large sections of the south side of the arena to easily obtain the travertine they burned for quicklime, an ingredient in mortar. The mortar to build walls made of hand-sized stones was more valuable than the massive quarried blocks that would have proved difficult, if not impossible, to transport to a new building site.

The first Basilica of St. Peter, as well as all other early Christian churches in Rome (fig. 4.1), was constructed mainly from the materials of Roman buildings. Columns from the Forum of Trajan and its Basilica Ulpia were carted across the city to provide the four rows of columns separating the nave and side aisles at old St. Peter's. The survival of Hadrian's Pantheon can be attributed to its conversion to the Christian church of Santa Maria ad Martyres in the seventh century rather than from admiration of it as the most impressive surviving Roman building in the city (see fig. 1.16). During the Renaissance, many Roman buildings that had survived relatively intact were scavenged for new construction. Cardinal Riario's magnificent palazzo, later named the Cancelleria, is made of cut stone from the ruins of many Roman buildings including the Theater of Pompey, formerly located mere blocks away (fig. 4.3).

Modern issues of preservation are extremely complex and reflect cultural values and worldwide involvement with those buildings considered of extreme significance. Current approaches to the handling of the past arose from an appreciation of history, both local and national, that had its beginnings in the eighteenth century and grew in intensity in the nineteenth century in Europe and, finally, in America. No single approach to the appreciation of the past existed then or now.

The extremes in attitude can be seen in the early efforts in Britain and France. The range spanned from the conservation of a building in its dilapidated state as espoused by John Ruskin (1819–1900), the most influential polemicist of mid-nineteenth-century Britain, to the re-creation of a building in a fashion better than it had ever existed as promoted by the French writer and architect Eugène Viollet-le-Duc (1814–1879). Both views express a valuation of the past and both continue to find adherents in current practice, although a middle ground is more often the dominant position.

Preservation efforts in Britain began with zealous interventions in Gothic churches in the early nineteenth century that spread to a nationwide enthusiasm for improving Anglican buildings dating originally from the Middle Ages to fit current religious practices. The churches were not only stabilized from further deterioration, but were often altered to enhance useful function. In reaction to this alteration of what he considered the beauty and value of age, Ruskin was vehement. In his influential work *The Seven Lamps of Architecture*, he wrote:

Architecture is to be regarded by us with the most serious thought. We may live without her, and worship without her, but we cannot remember without her. How cold is all history, how lifeless all imagery, compared to that which the living nation writes, and the uncorrupted marble bears!—how many

[4.4] *The exterior of Uppark, a National Trust property located southwest of London, in its restored condition following a fire in 1989. The facade remains essentially unchanged from its construction in 1690.*
National Trust of Britain

pages of doubtful record might we not often spare, for a few stones left one upon another! . . . And if indeed there be any profit in our knowledge of the past, or any joy in the thought of being remembered hereafter, which can give strength to present exertion, or patience to present endurance, there are two duties respecting national architecture whose importance it is impossible to overrate: the first, to render the architecture of the day, historical; and, the second, to preserve, as the most precious of inheritances, that of past ages.[1]

In 1877, concerned with the removal of inconsistent elements in medieval buildings, William Morris and other members of the Pre-Raphaelite Brotherhood established the Society for the Protection of Ancient Buildings. After an uncertain beginning, the organization grew from its original focus of medieval monumental buildings to encompass vernacular and high-style buildings and entire cityscapes. Additional interest groups were founded in the twentieth century to address preservation issues for periods of buildings that Morris could never have conceived as worthy of preservation. Among these preservations groups are the Georgian Group (1937), the Victorian Society (1958), and the Thirties (later renamed Twentieth Century) Society (1979).

The establishment of the National Trust in 1895 was of great significance to the preservation movement in Britain. The charitable organization was formed to receive gifts of buildings, coastline, and countryside, and to protect these properties from destruction. The first protected buildings predated 1600 and reflected concern for the imminent loss of architectural heritage if the buildings had been demolished. In 1937, Parliament passed an act providing for the Trust's acquisition of country houses. With this expansion of their acquisitions, many of the most notable private classical residences in Britain have been preserved in perpetuity and are now accessible by the public.

A significant example of the preservation efforts of the National Trust is evident in Uppark, the estate of the Meade-Fetherstonhaugh family, who passed the property to the Trust in 1954. The family continued to occupy the upper floor, and the main floor and estate grounds were opened to public visits (fig. 4.4). On August 30, 1989, an extensive fire damaged the state rooms of the main floor and obliterated the family apartments on the upper floor (fig. 4.5). The relatively low height of the main floor above the ground and the large French doors opening onto terraces enabled the valiant staff, volunteers, and Meade-Fetherstonhaugh family members to repeatedly enter the burning house to save the majority of furnishings and decorations. The dilemma about what to do with the severely damaged building came down to three options: demolish the surviving shell of the building; preserve the shell as a ruin; or restore the building.[2] After much deliberation, the decision was made to restore Uppark as closely as possible to its original condition and incorporate much the surviving materials (fig. 4.5). Fortuitously, the important engravings of the Print Room, c. 1770, had been removed for restoration at the time of the fire (see fig. 2.5).

The Trust commissioned writers Christopher Rowell and John Martin Robinson to record the restoration process in *Uppark Restored* (1996). Commenting on the project as a training ground for craftsmen, the authors wrote:

> The Uppark project engaged talent of high calibre; it also went some way to heal the damaging rift between the building industry and craftsmen, artists and conservators. For the young craftsmen, especially the woodcarvers and plasterers,

it was a chance to measure themselves alongside eighteenth-century work of superb quality. For the Trust it was an opportunity to extend its policy of reviving and nurturing the crafts and skills required in the upkeep of its historic properties and collections.[3]

Extensive fires at many other architectural treasures also furthered the revitalization of building crafts throughout Europe. Properties requiring major repairs include Hampton Court Palace (1986), Windsor Castle (1992), and La Fenice Opera House in Venice (1996) (figs. 4.6, 7; 6.4). Among the many restorations required to repair war damage incurred between 1941 and 1944, the examples of Pavlovsk Palace in St. Petersburg and Frauenkirche in Dresden are exceptional (figs. 4.8–11). In each of these cases of fire or war damage, the decision was made to restore the building compatibly with its original appearance rather than rebuilding in a current modernist style. The decision promoted the building crafts and knowledge of classical architecture.

HISTORIC PRESERVATION IN AMERICA

Concern for the preservation of cultural heritage also developed in America in the nineteenth century; however, private individuals were the ones to take action. An organized governmental preservation plan would not appear until the twentieth century. In 1853, the Mount Vernon Ladies' Association was organized to rescue the threatened home of George Washington. In 1858, without the assistance of the state of Virginia

[4.6] *In 1992, Windsor Castle incurred extensive damage during a fire. The ceiling of the Crimson Drawing Room collapsed and the marquetry floor was damaged beyond repair. The firm of Donald Insall & Associates received numerous awards for their lead in the restoration of the Crimson Drawing Room, which included re-creation of the plaster ceiling, a new floor, and installation of new hand-woven silk curtains and wall linings.* Royal Collection Trust / © Her Majesty Queen Elizabeth II 2013

[4.7] *La Fenice, Venice's world-renowned opera house, suffered devastating fires in 1774, 1836, and 1996 that each required complete rebuilding. Although the restoration team was led by the modernist Italian architect Aldo Rossi (1931–1997), the most recent reconstruction restored the house to its nineteenth-century appearance.*

[4.8 OPPOSITE] *Pavlovsk Palace (1780–1825), St. Petersburg, Russia, suffered extensive damage during the nine-hundred-day siege of the city by the German army during World War II. With only the principal walls remaining, the palace was reconstructed to its original appearance. The Grecian Room includes a colonnade of Corinthian columns with fluted verdi antico shafts, monumental fireplaces faced with lapis lazuli and jasper, and exquisitely detailed plaster moldings.*

[4.9 ABOVE] *The city of Dresden, Germany, was destroyed by Allied bombers in raids from February 13 to 14, 1945. Following the war, main parts of the city and monumental cultural buildings were restored to their historic appearance.*

[4.10 ABOVE] *The ruins of the Baroque Lutheran church in Dresden, the Frauenkirche (c. 1743), remained as a symbol of the effects of war until it was fully restored through private British and German funding efforts. All extant pieces of the original building were reused in the reconstructed church and are recognizable as the dark-toned stone.*

[4.11 FOLLOWING PAGES] *From 1998 to 2005, the interior of the Frauenkirche was restored to its prewar appearance.*

[4.12] *The two-story Large Dining Room at Mount Vernon was restored and repainted in 1981. The bold coloration was a favorite of George Washington's. The twenty-four dining chairs were made by Philadelphia cabinetmaker John Aitken. Details of pastoral life in the marble chimneypiece (installed 1786) may have inspired the motifs of crops and tools that decorate the walls and ceiling.*

or the federal government, the recently established nonprofit organization purchased the derelict house from John Augustine Washington III and opened it for public visits in 1860. The Association continues to oversee the most popular house museum in America and, after thorough research, restored its original brilliant interior colors (fig. 4.12). In 1864 the federal government purchased the Virginia home of Robert E. Lee, but the decision to make this first federal purchase of a historic property was based more on wartime retribution than concern for the preservation of Arlington House.

John D. Rockefeller and Dr. W. A. R. Goodwin initiated Colonial Williamsburg in the late 1920s, the largest privately funded restoration project in the country. Their intent was to re-create the appearance of the city as it looked in the period when Williamsburg was the largest and wealthiest British colony in America. The work not only prevented the loss of valuable eighteenth-century architecture, but it encouraged the development of cultural and artistic knowledge and the training of skilled craftsmen to implement the restoration of architecture, art, and furnishings. The most architecturally impressive residence in Colonial Williamsburg had been the Governor's Palace (fig. 4.13). Construction had begun in 1706 and extensive additions had been made as late as 1752. In December 1781 the impressive Georgian residence was destroyed by fire. By this time the capital of Virginia had been relocated to Richmond, and the palace remained a ruin until the 1930s. Faithful re-creation was made possible by written descriptions and a measured floor plan drawn by Thomas Jefferson in 1779.

In the 1930s, the nation's understanding of preservation changed through both local and federal efforts. In 1931, Charleston, South Carolina, became the first historic district established through local legislation to protect its wealth of fine public buildings and private residences (fig. 4.14).

[4.15] *The Supreme Court Historical Society (founded in 1974) was headquartered in a nineteenth-century building that had suffered a renovation in the 1950s giving the building an inaccurate appearance of a Federal-style town house.*

[4.16] *The firm of Allan Greenberg Architect altered the facade of the Supreme Court Historical Society to create a dignified classical building more in keeping with the surrounding context of the Capitol Hill Historic District of Washington, D.C.*

[4.17 OPPOSITE] *The new sitting room of the Supreme Court Historical Society was part of the renovation by Allan Greenberg Architect.*

In 1937, the French Quarter in New Orleans was also established as a historic district. During the Depression, a number of government-sponsored programs supported the documentation of historic and threatened buildings. The most important of these programs still in existence is the Historic American Buildings Survey established in 1934 through the efforts of Charles Peterson, a young park service landscape architect. This program partnered the efforts of the National Park Service with the American Institute of Architects and the Library of Congress. The impetus was to create detailed records of threatened buildings that represented the character of America from the smallest out building to the most monumental work and, at the same time, provide employment for skilled architects who were unable to find work during the Depression. The need to document America's architectural legacy survived the desperate economic times of the 1930s and the built heritage of the country continues to be recorded through this vital program.

Congress did not create a national organization to receive and preserve historic properties until 1949. The Act reads in part, "The purposes of the National Trust shall be to receive donations of sites, buildings, and objects significant in American history and culture, to preserve and administer them for public benefit, to accept, hold, and administer gifts . . . for the purpose of carrying out the preservation program . . ."[4] The National Trust is an advocacy group for the preservation of historic properties through education and the maintenance of a small number of properties that are significant to the wider culture of the nation.

The importance of preservation advocacy in the current era is critical to counteract damage incurred from modernist theory that proposed, as acceptable and laudable, the elimination of extant buildings and entire cities and replacing them with currently styled architecture. In 1925, the principal modern polemicist, Le Corbusier, proposed the "renewal" of Paris through his "Plan Voisin," which called for the

[4.20] *The Villa Torlonia, Rome (c. 1806, designed by Giuseppe Valadier) was occupied by Benito Mussolini from 1925 to 1943. Perhaps due to the building's connection to the Fascist dictator, the villa was left to deteriorate until its full restoration in the 1990s. The dome on pendentives in the ballroom hovers above a square room defined by colonnaded screens.* © Roma Capitale—Sovraintenze Bene Culturali: Musei di Villa Torlonia

[4.21] *The dining room of the Villa Torlonia is an oval shape decorated with sculpture in niches and multiple painted panels in the walls and ceiling. The villa is now owned and operated by the Municipality of Rome.* © Roma Capitale—Sovraintenze Bene Culturali: Musei di Villa Torlonia

removal of historic Paris north of the Seine and introducing glass skyscrapers in parklike settings. Following Cobusier's proposal and in the name of renewal, wholesale destruction of older sections of cities occurred across America, as well as less dramatic but equally negative replacement of historic urban facades with modern simplified treatments of glass and unornamented surfaces. In his book *Architecture in Context* (1980), Brent Brolin commented:

> The modernist architectural code of ethics maintained that history was irrelevant, that our age was unique and therefore our architecture must be cut off from the past. Just a few short decades ago modernists argued that everyone in the world, their tastes freed by the Movement, would soon want to live in the same kind of houses, in the same kind of modern cities, all of which would reflect the spirit of our times. (While the "times" were always "ours," the decision as to which forms characterized them was always "theirs," the architectural elite.) Because of this overwhelming belief several generations of architects have felt little need to accommodate their work to the older, theoretically obsolete architecture around it.[5]

The desire to maintain cultural complexity ensures that buildings of all periods will be maintained and restored and, oftentimes in the face of catastrophe, they will be reconstructed (figs. 4.15–21). The desire for preservation insures the continued need for architects trained in classical traditions and the skilled craftsmen essential to the creation of needed details.

Contemporary Restorations

A s indicated in the overview of preservation history in the preceding chapter, preservation includes both individual buildings
and entire cities. Numerous disciplines including architects,
engineers, historic preservationists, and archaeologists are involved with
ensuring the survival of their nation's built heritage. Preservation projects differ from new construction in the immense complexity of working
with existing building fabric. The four firms presented in this chapter
were selected to represent a range of preservation efforts from restoration, conservation, rehabilitation, and renovation for new use. The projects range from enhancing well-preserved buildings to re-creation after
devastating fires and stabilization following earthquake damage.

*John Milner restored the Jayne House in
Philadelphia to its original use as a single-
family house. The two-and-a-half-story
entrance hall is the focus of the design.*

JOHN MILNER
ARCHITECTS

John Milner Architects is among the most respected preservation firms in the United States. From offices in Chadds Ford and Philadelphia, Pennsylvania, their international architectural practice specializes in the restoration, preservation, and conservation of all manner of buildings from national historic landmarks to vernacular farmsteads, and also in the design of new residences inspired by American and European architectural traditions. Milner founded his practice in 1968 and shares design responsibilities with three other principals, Mary Werner DeNadai, Christina Carter, and Christopher Miller. Recalling his decision to enter the field of historic preservation, Milner wrote, "While studying architecture at The University of Pennsylvania, I served as a summer intern with the Historic American Buildings Survey. The world of period design and construction was opened to me, and became the foundation for my future work in preservation and design."[1] Since 1976, Milner has shared his knowledge with a generation of students as adjunct professor of architecture in the graduate program in historic preservation at the University of Pennsylvania. Lectures elucidating best practices in preservation, as well as the unique challenges associated with restoring old buildings, earned Milner the 2007 G. Holmes Perkins Award for Distinguished Teaching from the university.

Outstanding among the firm's preservation work in the classical tradition, the restoration of Nemours Mansion and Gardens in Wilmington, Delaware, received eight distinguished awards including the 2010 National Preservation Honor Award given by the National Trust for Historic Preservation. Built from 1910 to 1911 to the designs of the New York firm of Carrère and Hastings, the 47,000-square-foot Nemours was the home of Alfred I. duPont. The building's and family's histories formed the starting point for the preservation approach. The house, gardens, and outbuildings of the 225-acre estate were all addressed in the restoration plans. Structural problems were resolved; exterior and interior paint colors and faux finishes were studied meticulously by Frank S.

Welsh; mechanical systems and fire suppression systems were updated. Surprisingly, the large reception hall was made of Brandywine granite and covered with a thin layer of plaster scored and painted to resemble blocks of French limestone. During the restoration, the walls were refinished in a faux ashlar glaze, and each block was hand-painted to ensure that no two stones were alike.[2]

The Jayne House in Philadelphia is a significant surviving example of the work of celebrated Philadelphia architect Frank Furness (1839–1912). Built in 1895 at a prominent corner in Philadelphia's Rittenhouse Square neighborhood, the building served as the home of the architect's niece and her husband. In the 1940s, it was adapted as a synagogue, and the finishes in the entire north side of the first floor were removed to create one large worship space. The building housed various institutions until the current owners purchased the property with plans to restore its original function as a single-family residence. Despite the years of modifications, many original features survived, including the splendid two-and-one-half-story oak-paneled central hall crowned by a leaded-glass skylight. After removing a maze of 1980s office partitions, the architects reinterpreted new floor plans based on the original configuration and utilizing original interior wall and door locations wherever possible. The comprehensive restoration of the exterior included a new terracotta tile roof, full restoration and conservation of brick and terra-cotta masonry, and the restoration of ironwork throughout.

The firm also designs new houses drawn from the historic and environmental context of their settings. Their work in the Philadelphia region reflects Milner's extensive knowledge of historic forms gained from decades of work with the finest examples of eighteenth-, nineteenth-, and twentieth-century buildings, and their designs in American Georgian and Federal brick architecture have proven to have great appeal for clients in China.

NEMOURS MANSION AND GARDENS

Wilmington, Delaware
Original architects: Carrère and Hastings, 1909
Restoration and Renovation: 2004–2008

The Alfred I. duPont estate, with its 47,000-square-foot home designed by Carrère and Hastings and its immense gardens, was restored to its original beauty and given improved use as a house museum.

THE JAYNE HOUSE

Philadelphia, Pennsylvania
Original architects: Furness, Evans & Company, 1895
Restoration and Renovation: 2007–2010

The original building, designed in 1895 by Furness, Evans & Company, underwent many changes though the years including its transformation into a synagogue. From 2007 to 2010, the building was extensively renovated and restored to its original use as a single-family residence. The most spectacular space is the two-and-a-half-story central hall topped with a leaded-glass skylight.

NEW RESIDENCE

Near Philadelphia

This home was designed in the style of the late-colonial-period houses of southeastern Pennsylvania for owners with an important collection of early American fine furniture and decorative arts.

BRUNO AND ALEXANDRE
LAFOURCADE

Bruno Lafourcade is the founding partner in an international design practice located in Saint-Rémy-de-Provence, France. Founded in 1968, the firm specializes in the restoration of farmhouses, country manors, castles, hotels, and wineries. In the 1960s, when Lafourcade decided to pursue his passion for working with older buildings, architecture programs did not offer the training needed for skillful restoration and additions to historic structures. Through self-education and apprenticeship with an elderly mason, Lafourcade gained the knowledge and experience needed to work with the traditional materials of masonry bearing walls, carved stone, stucco, and heavy timber framing.

In 1970, his firm received the high honor of the Prix Nationale de Restauration for the restoration and renovation of a seventeenth-century Carthusian monastery in the Périgord region of France. Recognition of the quality of this project set the tone for the young firm's future work in restoration as well as new construction.

His approach to restoration involves careful study of the site—its microclimate, landscape features, and the character of the existing buildings he will work with—all concepts that have been the domain of architecture since the Romans inhabited Gaul. Concerning his approach to design and its difference from the approach of modern design, Lafourcade has said:

What we do is not the kind of thing they teach at the universities. At the universities, architects learn how to use computers. They do not learn taste, they do not learn charm, they do not learn culture. We build with the images we carry in our heads. We must know how the local winds blow, how a tree will protect a home in the summer, and how the mistral will blow off the surrounding hills in winter. Then we must listen to the client as carefully as a doctor making a diagnosis. Do they have dogs? Do they love music? Do they love flowers? You are not merely designing a residence, you are creating a way of life.[1]

The firm's work has been the subject of numerous awards. In 1989, Jack Lang, the French minister of culture, awarded Bruno Lafourcade the title of Chevalier de l'Ordre des Arts et des Lettres for his contributions to the arts of France. In 2010, a client of Lafourcade in the north of Europe received the Prix Prince Louis de Polignac for the brilliant restoration of his Château de France, a restoration by Bruno Lafourcade and his son, Alexandre.

Alexandre is now Bruno's design partner in the firm, while Dominique Lafourcade, Bruno's wife, is a recognized landscape designer and collaborates in the creation of the setting of their work. Their teamwork is evident in the projects that follow, including restoration of and additions to a manor house near Aix-en-Provence; a redesign and restoration of and gardens for a manor house near Saint-Rémy-de-Provence; and the extensive renovation of a château in the South of France.

FRENCH CHÂTEAU

South of France
Original building: Eighteenth century
Restoration and renovation: Completed 2008

New stuccoed walls and a decorative cartouche accenting the entrance introduce a refined quality to the original building. In the music room, an ancient stone fireplace in keeping with the original château was added. In the southern dining room, the original rotunda shape and woodwork have been restored and a marble fireplace added.

BRUNO AND ALEXANDRE LAFOURCADE

BRUNO AND ALEXANDRE LAFOURCADE

COUNTRY MANOR

Near Aix-en-Provence
Original building: Eighteenth century
Restoration and renovation: Completed 2003

An elegant new staircase fits harmoniously
within the existing building. The large salon is
organized around a massive stone chimneypiece.

BRUNO AND ALEXANDRE LAFOURCADE

COUNTRY MANOR HOUSE

Near Saint-Rémy-de-Provence
Original building: Eighteenth century
Restoration and renovation: Completed 2003

These original farm buildings from the eighteenth century were transformed into a stately residence through the reworking of the facade with a pedimented entrance, new windows, and shutters. The south facade of the farm building before its transformation is seen above.

ARCHITECTURAL RESOURCES GROUP

Founded in 1980 during the nascent stage of the historic preservation movement, Architectural Resources Group remains at the forefront of protecting, adapting, and adding to some of the country's most beloved buildings and landscapes through the intertwining disciplines of planning, architectural design, and conservation. From its origins as a preservation firm, Architectural Resources Group's practice has evolved to include significantly broader planning considerations for historic sites and multi-structure campuses as well as the development of designs for new additions and new freestanding buildings that beautifully complement their historic environments.

Architectural Resources Group began in a small office in San Francisco's North Beach neighborhood, where Bruce Judd and Stephen Farneth partnered to form the practice. Today the firm's headquarters are located at Pier 9 on the Embarcadero in San Francisco, with additional offices in Pasadena and Portland, Oregon.

Over the years, both men became nationally recognized experts in the historic preservation field. Judd served on the President's National Advisory Council for Historic Preservation, on the US Senate's expert panel to review plans for the Capitol and its grounds, as president of San Francisco Architectural Heritage, and on the board of the California Preservation Foundation.

Farneth earned a bachelor of architecture degree at Carnegie Mellon University and a certificate in architectural conservation from the highly respected International Centre for the Study of the Preservation and Restoration of Cultural Property, in Rome. He served on the executive committee of the State Historic Building Safety Board in California and helped to rewrite the California State Historic Building Code. He also served as the vice chairman of the board of trustees of the US committee of the International Council on Monuments and Sites.

Today the leadership at Architectural Resources Group includes Farneth at the helm, with principals Aaron Jon Hyland and Naomi Miroglio overseeing architecture and preservation, and Charles Edwin Chase as principal of planning and David P. Wessel as principal of conservation.

The firm's achievements have been recognized with more than one hundred awards in design excellence, conservation, and planning from the National Trust for Historic Preservation, the American Institute of Architects, the California Governor's Office, and the California Preservation Foundation. In 2006, the AIA California Council named Architectural Resources Group their Firm of the Year, the organization's highest honor. The award recognizes firms that consistently produce distinguished work for a period of at least ten years as well as work that has transcended a singular area of expertise.

Much of the firm's success results from the belief that historic buildings can gracefully accommodate contemporary uses in ways that enrich the lives of those who occupy the buildings and the community at large. While Architectural Resources Group's portfolio includes many iconic historic structures, the majority of the firm's projects involve upgrading historic buildings that are simply contributors to the fabric of their era. Designed by the best architects of their generation, these buildings are solid, well-executed, institutional structures often with a high level of architectural detail. Architectural Resources Group works with clients to reuse these buildings in ways that preserve and enhance their gracious qualities, which revitalizes operations, energizes users and neighborhoods, and helps owners to understand and capitalize on the intrinsic value of their assets.

STANFORD UNIVERSITY MUSEUM OF ART

(now the Iris and B. Gerald Cantor Center for Visual Arts)
Stanford University
Stanford, California
Original architects: Percy and Hamilton with Ernest J. Ransome, 1894
Rehabilitation: Completed 1994

The founders of Stanford University, Leland and Jane Lathrop Stanford, named the original building the Leland Stanford Junior Museum in memory of their son. Structural damage caused by the 1989 Loma Prieta earthquake required this early example of reinforced concrete to be extensively repaired.

GARRETT HALL

University of Virginia
Frank Batten School of Leadership and Public Policy
Charlottesville, Virginia
Original architects: McKim, Mead and White, 1908
Rehabilitation: Completed 2011

The historic central dining hall or refectory building was adapted for new uses as classrooms and conference spaces. The original two-story lobby space, closed in 1959, was reconstructed based on historic drawings.

ARCHITECTURAL RESOURCES GROUP

164

CECIL H. GREEN LIBRARY

Stanford University
Stanford, California
Original architects: John Bakewell and Arthur Brown, 1919
Rehabilitation: Completed 1992

After the 1989 Loma Prieta earthquake, the 1919 Green Library designed by Bakewell & Brown was severely damaged. Structural and building systems were upgraded to conform to new earthquake standards while respecting the historic quality of the building.

HUNTINGTON ART GALLERY

San Marino, California
Original architects: Myron Hunt and Elmer Grey, 1911
Rehabilitation: Completed 2008

Built as a lavish residence for railroad magnate Henry E. Huntington, the Huntington Art Gallery exhibits his extensive collection of European art, rare books, and plant specimens in the property's botanical gardens. Interior and exterior finishes were restored and new gallery spaces expanded the exhibition capacity of the house museum.

PASADENA CITY HALL

Pasadena, California
Original architects: Bakewell and Brown, 1927
Restoration: Completed 2007

The historic city hall designed by the significant firm of partners
John Bakewell and Arthur Brown was restored over a twenty-year
period through the retrofitting of all structural and mechanical systems and restoration of the exterior plaster and cast stone facade.

DONALD INSALL
ASSOCIATES

Founded in 1958, the firm of Donald Insall Associates provides an array of architectural, historic building, and planning services from its eight offices across the United Kingdom. Knighted in 2010 for his life's work in architectural conservation, founder Sir Donald Insall received his education in architecture and conservation during and immediately following World War II. As a Lethaby Scholar of the Society for the Protection of Ancient Buildings, he expanded his traditional architectural training to include the hands-on study of building materials and the reasons for their decay and need for renewal. Of this period of training, Insall has written:

> As Lethaby Scholars, we came to see how each place and structure we may strive to save is alive and constantly changing. For every building is a product not only of its original generator—whether architect or builder, caravanist or monk—but of the continuing effects upon its materials of time and weather, and of generations of successive occupants, each with his own set of values and requirements. Each building carries, and clearly demonstrates, the impact and influence of all its changing and unforeseeable circumstances.[1]

During Insall's long career as an architect, planner, and writer, the modern field of architectural conservation in Britain has been, in large measure, shaped by his efforts. He was a founding commissioner of the Historic Buildings and Monuments Commission for England (more commonly known simply as English Heritage), established in 1983 to supervise over four hundred historic sites in England. His professional work informed his understanding of the varied needs of historic sites supervised by English Heritage from Stonehenge (c. 2400 BCE) to Chiswick House (1729), to Eltham Palace (completed during the 1930s).

Through his writing, Insall has been able to share his knowledge of conservation issues developed through the professional work of his office. In addition to numerous articles and reports, he has written two books, *The Care of Old Buildings Today* (1972) and *Living Buildings—Architectural Conservation: Philosophy, Principles and Practice* (2008), which celebrated the fiftieth year of the architectural firm that he founded. His books have not only provided cogent outlines of conservation issues and techniques, but they also show examples of the firm's projects which demonstrate the breadth of historic architecture in the United Kingdom.

Among the firm's well-known projects is the post-fire restoration of Windsor Castle from 1992 to 1997. Donald Insall Associates served as coordinating architects for the restoration, which involved a team of some 1,500 contractors and craftsmen to re-create lost details, restore historic fabric where possible, and create new structure where needed. The principal state rooms were severely damaged by the water required to extinguish the flames as well as by the fire itself. The ceiling of the Crimson Drawing Room had collapsed, but after careful study its interiors were restored to the late-1820s designs of King George IV's furniture makers Morel & Seddon, who created the stunning gilded wall paneling and crimson silk interiors.

Throughout the firm's long history, Donald Insall Associates has shaped the direction of architectural conservation in Britain. The exceptional quality of its projects to conserve the historic fabric of the country has been recognized with over 160 national and international awards and commendations, including ten for the restoration of Windsor Castle. Sir Donald Insall remains a consultant to the firm, whose chairman is now Nicholas Thompson.

WINDSOR CASTLE

Windsor, England
Original building: c. 1070 to present
Fire Restoration: 1992–1997

After an almost total destruction by the 1992 fire, the Crimson Drawing Room was restored to its 1830 appearance. Above is a detail of the restored carved and gilded ornament, originally removed from Carlton House, London, to the Crimson Drawing Room at Windsor Castle for King George IV in 1830.

TOWN HALL

Liverpool, England
Original building: John Wood the Elder, 1749–1754
New interiors by James Wyatt from 1795
Refurbished: 1991–1994

A surviving colored elevation by James Wyatt from 1805
was used to guide the redecoration of the Dining Room.

MANSION HOUSE

London
Original architect: George Dance the Elder, 1739–1752
Refurbished: 1991–1993

The building was constructed as the official residence of the Lord Mayor of London. The original open courtyard from 1752 was roofed over in 1862 and used as the Salon. The refurbishment included a new Doric entablature, coved ceiling, and octagonal roof light.

DONALD INSALL ASSOCIATES

CHAPTER FIVE

The Revival of Modern Classicism through Education of Designers and Craftsmen

Elizabeth Meredith Dowling

[5.1] *Allan Greenberg's transformation of spaces within the modernist 1960s State Department Building are evident in the axial view from the east reception hall through the Treaty Room.* Photograph by Richard Cheek, courtesy the Diplomatic Reception Rooms, U.S. Department of State, Washington, D.C.

[5.2] *One of four variations of carved consoles in the Treaty Room designed by Allan Greenberg Architect.* Photograph by Richard Cheek, courtesy the Diplomatic Reception Rooms, U.S. Department of State, Washington, D.C.

[5.3 OPPOSITE] *In the elliptical Treaty Room, designed by Allan Greenberg Architect, subtle rhythms develop in the room from the patterned floor made of inlaid maple, ebony, and mahogany to the walls accented with paired Corinthian columns.* Photograph by Richard Cheek, courtesy the Diplomatic Reception Rooms, U.S. Department of State, Washington, D.C.

The survival of classical architecture beyond the mid-twentieth century is indebted to two interconnected streams—the preservation movement and the revival of classical education. These movements provided the training of designers and the employment for skilled craftsmen whose knowledge would, otherwise, have been completely lost. Total interruption of the flow of knowledge from master to apprentice, whether in architecture or building crafts, would have made the continuation of traditions most unlikely. Although the techniques of classical design were not "secret," as had been the case in medieval craft guilds, knowledge not handed down through design firms or craft companies had to be reacquired. The search for lost design methods, detailed knowledge of proportion in design, the assembly of moldings, and so on has demanded immense dedication on the part of all involved in the production of fine traditional architecture. This chapter addresses the revival of classical education in architecture, interior design, and the building crafts, as well as the creation of new professional organizations that support the mission of fine traditional design.

[5.5 OPPOSITE] *In 1984, John Blatteau designed the Benjamin Franklin Dining Room in the State Department Building. The new design replaced the 1950s dropped ceiling and expanses of glass walls that still exist behind the twenty freestanding scagliola columns.*

[5.4] *Office of the deputy secretary of state in the State Department Building, designed by Allan Greenberg Architect.* Photograph by Richard Cheek, courtesy the Diplomatic Reception Rooms, U.S. Department of State, Washington, D.C.

REVIVAL OF CLASSICAL ARCHITECTURE

In the 1950s and 1960s few classical designers continued to find work, and those who did usually had small, predominantly residential practices. Philip Trammell Shutze and James Means in Georgia, A. Hays Town in Louisiana, and Raymond Erith in Britain are characteristic of this group of classical survivors. The advent of a reinvigorated classical movement occurred gradually over some thirty years, beginning in the late 1980s. During this time educational support developed through the influence of Charles, Prince of Wales, in Britain, and the School of Architecture at the University of Notre Dame in the United States.

During the transition from Beaux-Arts training to modern classicism, a unique project displayed the desire by both architects and clients to restore principles of classical beauty to the profession of architecture—principles that, in America, had been overshadowed by the influence of modernist theory. In 1961, the State Department in Washington, D.C., opened its new Brutalist-style headquarters and, immediately, a movement was initiated by Clement E. Conger, curator of the Diplomatic Reception Rooms, to transform the simple modern spaces of the eighth floor into a display of the artistic heritage of the United States. As Paul Goldberger commented, "The most charitable thing that could be said about the sprawling, limestone-clad headquarters of the United States Department

[5.6] *In 1991, Alvin Holm designed the Nineteenth-Century European Painting and Sculpture Galleries at the Metropolitan Museum of Art, New York City, in a manner most fitting for the art collection. By creating pure classical details rather than caricatures of classical elements, Holm broke with the current postmodern trend.*

of State in Washington, D.C., is that it is a credible period piece from the late 1950s. It is also utterly banal, institutional, and graceless, suggesting the dreariness of bureaucracy more then the dignity of diplomacy."[1]

Several architects contributed their talent to the creation of this new suite of public rooms intended as a backdrop for events conducted by the secretary of state and other members of the cabinet and the vice president. From 1965 to 1980, Georgia architect Edward Vason Jones transformed a stark modern interior into a sequence of delicately scaled, civilized rooms for the diplomatic receptions of heads of state, foreign ministers, and distinguished foreign and American guests. After Jones's death, Allen Greenberg continued the transformation of the modernist interiors, as he described, into "rooms to reflect the continuity of American diplomacy and embody the noblest ideals of American life and culture."[2] From 1983 to 1989, the offices of the secretary and deputy secretary of state and the Treaty Room suite introduced an eighteenth-century aura to the otherwise nondescript building (figs. 5.1–4). Greenberg drew inspiration from American design, but, as is possible with the elastic language of classical design, transformed the precedents to convey clearer nationalistic symbolism. In the tradition of Benjamin Latrobe's Tobacco Leaf Capital for the Senate rotunda, Greenberg created a Corinthian derivation he terms the Great Seal Order, after the secretary of state's role as custodian of the nation's seal.

In 1984, John Blatteau was selected as architect for the Benjamin Franklin Dining Room, located in the State Department Building. In the largest ceremonial room outside of the Capitol and the White House, Blatteau created a venue for dinners and receptions equal in refinement to the spaces available to European diplomats in their home countries (fig. 5.5). The scheme incorporates twenty freestanding and twelve engaged Corinthian scagliola columns, a majestic fireplace, and draped windows inserted within the floor plate of a 1960s office building. One can hardly imagine some of the nation's most important diplomatic dinners and receptions occurring in this building had it not been transformed from its original Brutalist design.

Another major public project indicating the continued respect for classical architecture involved the renovation of a major gallery at the Metropolitan Museum of Art in New York City. In 1991, with the bequest of Walter Annenberg's personal collection, plans already underway to renovate the Nineteenth-Century European Paintings and Sculpture Galleries were adjusted so the collection could be exhibited as a unit within the museum's extant collections (fig. 5.6).[3] Alvin Holm, whose office was in Philadelphia, was known to the curators of the nineteenth-century collection through courses he taught on classical design at the National Academy of Design in New York City. Although trained as a modernist, Holm had established his own architectural practice in restoration and new traditional design in 1976 and was, therefore, far more knowledgeable than most architects of the period in working within the Beaux-Arts tradition. Concerning the radical decision being made at a major art museum to reject currently popular architectural trends in favor of classicism, Gary Tinterow, Engelhard Curator of European Paintings, wrote:

THE ANNENBERG COLLECTION

In giving these rooms a classical appearance, we rejected the Post-Modern approach to historical ornament. We did not feel obliged to enlarge moldings or otherwise distort the classical canon in order to remind viewers that the Modern movement had severed ties with the past. As a repository of man's material culture from all ages and cultures, the Museum was entitled, we felt, to use the classical vocabulary legitimately and without apology, as it had in the past. In doing so, we sought to create noble spaces that are sober and restrained, spaces that recede sufficiently to allow the paintings and sculpture to be seen comfortably, without distraction. We set out to build well-proportioned Beaux-Arts paintings galleries such as those we thought the Museum had had at the beginning of the century. In fact, they had never been built. So we re-created the past we wished we had had.[4]

CLASSICAL EDUCATION IN ARCHITECTURE AND BUILDING CRAFTS

By the 1980s, two generations of young architects had received modernist academic training and lacked the foundation needed to create historically inspired design. Commenting on this lack of attention to classical knowledge in current architecture curricula, Robert A. M. Stern wrote:

> Without a meaningful program of professional education within the architecture schools themselves, Classicism cannot resume its role as a transferable discipline for the practitioners of the future. Imagine a university that would call itself serious but not have a Classics Department. Yet, in almost all architecture schools today, the Classical tradition is virtually ignored, its history barely addressed in broad surveys; and its language, the grammar and syntax that have structured every Western stylistic movement since the Renaissance, including early or so-called canonic Modernism itself, is completely ignored.[5]

The architects and designers from Europe and America whose work appears in this book demonstrate the variety of classical training gained outside formal architectural education through apprenticeship and self-guided study. Among the current practitioners in this book, only Allan Greenberg and Juan Pablo Molyneux received Beaux-Arts grounding in classical design—Greenberg through his education at the University of Witwatersrand in Johannesburg, South Africa, and Molyneux through his classes at the Ecole des Beaux-arts and the Ecole du Louvre in Paris. In the last decades of

[5.7 OPPOSITE] *"Leogane Civic Center, Southeast Elevation," part of the graduate thesis of Stephanie Anne Arrienda Jazmines, University of Notre Dame, 2011*

[5.8] *"Leogane Civic Center, Section through City Hall," part of the graduate thesis of Stephanie Anne Arrienda Jazmines, University of Notre Dame, 2011*

the twentieth century, solitary professors passing on basic knowledge of traditional principles offered random university courses in classical and traditional design.[6] Finally, in 1989, the systematic teaching of classical design was reintroduced in the architecture program at the University of Notre Dame under the leadership of its new director, Thomas Gordon Smith. Earlier Smith had taught a single course in classical principles at the University of Illinois in Chicago, but Smith's position at Notre Dame, in concert with the design faculty, offered the opportunity to develop a form of training not seen for fifty years.[7]

The program at the University of Notre Dame is not a revival of old methods of design instruction; instead a modern curriculum that represents an inclusive rather than exclusive viewpoint prepares students for contemporary practice. Consideration of context as an appropriate urban response is emphasized in studio problems. This understanding is further honed by the requirement that undergraduates spend a year and graduate students remain for a semester at Notre Dame's school located in the historic heart of Rome. There the students are immersed in analyzing the character of a historic city and learn by example how design successfully enhances urban life. This sensitivity to contextual design is an obvious characteristic of the work of all of the program's

graduates (figs. 5.7, 8). The curriculum balances topics like modern structural systems with knowledge of traditional forms of construction including masonry-bearing walls. Such inclusive knowledge allows the selection of sustainable and environmentally appropriate materials and systems based on a deeper understanding of their underlying principles, rather than merely relying on the current choices at hand. The students are also taught drawing, watercolor rendering, and computer-aided drafting, maintaining a balance of current and time-honored techniques.

Instruction in interior design was included in the education of the architect from the nineteenth through most of the twentieth century. The careful detailing of interiors necessitated knowledge of historic elements. The interior of a building was a harmonious reflection of its exterior character; however, as modernism focused on new materials and structural systems, as well as new complex buildings including hospitals, airports, and skyscrapers, the ability to control both the body and the soul of a building was abandoned. Interior design was resolved through the application of large sheets of glass and plain unornamented wall surfaces or, more recently, to extremely convoluted but unornamented surfaces. Detailing a traditional interior became a personally acquired skill, not fundamental knowledge shared by all

THE REVIVAL OF MODERN CLASSICISM

190

architects. In the Notre Dame program, however, presentation drawings of a design problem include detailed sketches of interiors (fig. 5.9). The program also offers an elective course in furniture design that includes the study of period furniture and the actual construction of a piece of furniture (fig. 5.10). With the requirement for professional registration of interior designers, many colleges in the United States offer degrees in interior design, but the focus of these programs principally addresses modernism. Knowledge of traditional design is assisted by courses on the history of furniture and architecture, but the greater knowledge is acquired through apprenticeship with established classical interior design firms and self-directed education.

Throughout the world, the training of craftsmen continues in the time-honored tradition of the apprentice learning from the master of any number of building crafts, but there is also a four-year college degree available in America. In 1989, Hurricane Hugo damaged many historic structures in Charleston, South Carolina. When numerous craftsmen were needed for repairs, it became clear that the city did not have enough local talent to carry out the work. Through the initial efforts of John Paul Huguley, many committed individuals sought to remedy the need for additional skilled workers through the founding in 1989 of the American College of the Building Arts (ACBA) in Charleston. In 2005, ACBA opened its doors, offering two degrees that provide training in architectural stone, forged architectural ironwork, preservation masonry, timber framing, carpentry, and plaster working, along with traditional liberal arts coursework. ACBA is the first institution in the United States to offer the combi-

[5.9 OPPOSITE]
"Grecian Parlor Perspective View," freehand sketch by Clay Rokicki for his thesis project, "A Decorative Arts Museum for New York City," University of Notre Dame, 2006 (thesis adviser Professor Norman Crowe)

[5.10] *"Window Bench" project for furniture class at Notre Dame designed and made by Elizabeth Slaski*

THE REVIVAL OF MODERN CLASSICISM

nation of applied and liberal arts, broadening the scope for future building artisans by equipping them with a wider knowledge of business, design, history, mathematics, English, science, drafting, and the arts. The school is housed in the Old Charleston City Jail of 1802, originally designed by Robert Mills. The graduates of the ACBA will increase the numbers of craftsmen in America exponentially by becoming masters in the training of additional skilled workers in the future.

In the 1980s in Great Britain, a similar disenchantment with modernism became a formal movement. The Prince of Wales was the leading voice in the growing concern with the urban failures of modernism. In 1988, BBC Television produced *A Vision of Britain*, which focused on the Prince's opinions regarding the impact of modern architecture on the character of historic sites, especially Paternoster Square, a 1960s urban development surrounding St. Paul's Cathedral in London. A year later, the program's information was published as a book by the same name and authored by Prince Charles, whose continuing interest in improving the quality of his country's urban life led to the creation of The Prince's Foundation for Building Community in 1998. The Prince's concern has been the maintenance of local culture in the face of the modernist cultural homogeneity. The Prince's Foundation directs efforts toward sustainable local architecture and urban traditions through a number of initiatives. Within the realm of education, the foundation supports a program for building crafts apprentices to enhance their knowledge; grad-

uate fellowships in sustainable architecture and urbanism; a summer school in traditional building; and a master of science in sustainable urban development offered at Oxford University. The emphasis on sustainability recognizes the need to observe the local culture and climate that has produced traditional architecture.

PROFESSIONAL SUPPORT AND RECOGNITION

By 1990, the college-aged student could now receive proper classical training from Notre Dame, but those architects already in practice desired educational opportunities as well. This void in professional education led Richard Ssammons, Richard Cameron, and Donald Rattner to imagine an organization that would function like the T-Square clubs of the 1920s.[8] In relating the origins of what would become the Institute of Classical Architecture and Art (ICA&A), Richard Cameron wrote:

In 1991 there was almost no place in New York for architects and designers to study the manual skills and intellectual foundations of classical architecture. We thought that there ought to be. It seemed such an obvious idea for those of us who had attempted to cobble together an education for ourselves with old books and the good luck of encountering great teachers here and there. We wanted to start a school of architecture

based on the old Beaux-Arts ideal of practicing architects teaching working students and we had the audacity to believe we could make such a school out of nothing more than our will. I think we probably thought it might take a couple of years. Ten years later, the Institute is both less than we ambitiously imagined and much more than we had any reason to hope.[9]

The Institute, like traditional and classical architecture, is flourishing. Its activities include courses, a yearly journal, and thematically focused study tours. The Institute's journal, *The Classicist*, includes peer-reviewed scholarly articles, student work, recently constructed buildings, and urban designs. Their first program, a six-week intensive summer course in New York City, continues to provide educational enrichment for students and professionals. Extensive offerings of shorter evening and weekend courses cover both basic and advanced information on classical design.[10] In addition, travel/study trips in Europe and America, exhibitions, and a lecture series of internationally known architects and historians occur regularly in the New York headquarters and in the fifteen chapters nationwide. In 2002, the Institute of Classical Architecture and Classical America, another nonprofit organization, merged to acknowledge the similarity of their missions and to draw strength from the combined organization. The Arthur Ross Awards, first given by Classical America in 1982 to Philip Trammell Shutze for architecture, continue as an annual award with the recently renamed Institute of Classical Architecture & Art. These awards recognize

life achievement in an array of areas including architecture, craftsmanship, landscape design, education, and stewardship. The Southeast Chapter of the ICA&A initiated recognition for excellence in current architecture, landscape design, and interior design in 2007 with the Philip Trammell Shutze Awards. Other chapters created their own awards program named for revered local classical architects. As of 2012, these programs included the Bulfinch Awards given by the Boston Chapter, the John Staub Awards given by the Texas Chapter, and the Addison Mizner Medal given by the Florida Chapter. The Institute also offers the Rieger Graham Prize to recent graduates of professional art and architecture programs. This award sponsors a three-month period of study at the American Academy in Rome.

Observing that professional architecture groups under the sway of modernist philosophy seldom recognize the able work of classical and traditional architects, Clem Labine created the Palladio Awards in 2002. Labine was an early supporter of traditional design through his development of two magazines, *Period Homes* and *Traditional Building*. Commenting on his naming the awards for Andrea Palladio, Labine wrote, "The name Palladio seemed a natural because he embodied the principles we wished to honor: Taking the best ideas and architectural precedents from the past and applying them in new ways so as to create humane, contemporary architecture that answers the needs of our time."[11] These awards continue to recognize individual current work in commercial, civic, and residential design.

The most significant international award based in the United States, the Richard H. Driehaus Prize for Classical Architecture, recognizes life achievement in the fields of classical and traditional architecture, or historic preservation (fig. 5.12). The prize of $200,000 doubles the monetary recognition of the formerly unmatched Pritzker Prize given for modern architecture. As of 2013, the winners include Léon Krier, Demetri Porphyrios, Quinlan Terry, Allan Greenberg, Jaquelin T. Robertson, Andrés Duany and Elizabeth Plater-Zyberk, Abdel-Wahed El-Wakil, Rafael Manzano Martos, Robert A. M. Stern, Michael Graves, and Thomas H. Beeby.

An outstanding example of the prizes awarded specifically to classical architecture, The Georgian Group recognizes exemplary conservation and restoration of Georgian buildings and landscapes in the United Kingdom, as well as new buildings located in Georgian contexts and new architecture in the classical tradition. The Georgian Group was founded in 1937 as a response to the destruction of significant Georgian buildings throughout Britain but especially in London.

The Philippe Rotthier European Prize for Architecture does not specifically reject modern design, but its principles of awarding urban designs that support the traditional city, the spirit of the place, and ecological design put traditional and classical architects in a more positive position since they share the values inherent in the award. Established in 1982, the first triennial award was given to Quinlan Terry for his design of Newfield House, in Yorkshire.

Contemporary Projects

The following section of the book present portfolios of currently practicing architects and designers followed by two essays. The portfolios of selected firms illustrate a variety of approaches employed to solve the needs for large and small residences, public buildings, and commercial projects.

The first of the two following essays "Ornament: A Source of Beauty," written by David Watkin, introduces the history of ornament as a defining element of classical architecture. The essential relationship between ornament and beauty contrasts with the twentieth-century theory given voice by Adolf Loos that the use of ornament in any form whether on one's person or in architecture is a primitive and obsolete activity in the modern world. The second essay "Proportion of Interiors," written by Richard Sammons, offers the reader an understanding of the complexity of classical design with its various ornamental details and size and shape of rooms all inextricably related in the most refined classical work.

Allan Greenberg designed the elegantly detailed surround for the dining room of his Georgian-Style House, New Jersey.

ALLAN GREENBERG
ARCHITECT

Allan Greenberg is an accomplished architect, historian, and writer whose approach to architecture is rooted in the relationship between politics and aesthetics. His fascination with eighteenth- and nineteenth-century American architecture is related to their genesis in the American Revolution and their architects' commitment to expressing American democratic ideals in architectural form. He has eloquently recorded his thoughts in both his article "The Architecture of Democracy" and his book *George Washington Architect*.[1]

Greenberg's background differs from other architects who appear to share his sensibilities—he was trained in both classicism and modernism, and sees no contradiction in admiring the architecture of Jefferson and Lutyens along with that of modern masters like Le Corbusier and Alvar Aalto, or in his experience working with Jørn Utzon during the design phase of the Sydney Opera House. Greenberg regards himself as a modern architect, not a traditionalist, who is committed to a renaissance of the political idealism that created the American Revolution and the architecture of that period.

Allan Greenberg was born in Johannesburg, South Africa, and his architectural education at the University of Witwatersrand included drawing the historic models of classical and Gothic architecture from memory.[2] He came to the United States to study under Paul Rudolph at Yale, where he received his master of architecture degree in 1965. His architecture is both exquisitely detailed and employs the most current construction techniques. On this topic he wrote, "Though Modernism claims to have brought technology to architecture, in fact it had been fully absorbed into the fabric of American classical architecture before the end of the 19th century. Classical architecture forged a new synthesis between the building industry and technology that revolutionized both the fabrication of materials and construction technology; it has always responded to the needs of architecture, current and future, at the same time reinterpreting the past and drawing it into the present."[3]

In 1972, Greenberg established his firm, which currently has offices in New York City; Alexandria, Virginia; and Greenwich, Connecticut. Greenberg's firm has attracted apprentice architects from around the world including Ernesto Buch and Francis Terry, both of whose work is included in this book. In addition to architectural practice, Greenberg has taught at Yale University's architecture and law schools, the University of Pennsylvania, and the division of Historic Preservation at Columbia University's Graduate School of Architecture, Planning, and Preservation. Because most schools do not prepare their students to work in classical design, his office has provided such training to many young architects and teachers. Today classical design is taught at the University of Notre Dame, where Greenberg's son Peter trained, and the University of Miami under Dean Elizabeth Plater-Zyberk, one of Greenberg's students when he taught at Yale.

Greenberg's work includes public, commercial, and institutional buildings as well as an extensive residential portfolio. His practice spans historic restoration, renovation, interior design services, and new construction. Greenberg's contributions to architecture through his design work, his writing, and his public lectures have received frequent recognition including the two most prestigous awards in traditional architecture, the Arthur Ross Award for Architecture, in 1990, and the Richard H. Driehaus Prize for Classical Architecture, which he was the first American to receive, in 2006.

A GEORGIAN-STYLE HOUSE

New Jersey
2005

ALLAN GREENBERG ARCHITECT

200

WATERFRONT RESIDENCE

Long Island Sound
1999

ALLAN GREENBERG ARCHITECT

FARMHOUSE IN CONNECTICUT

Connecticut
1986

ALLAN GREENBERG ARCHITECT

ALLAN GREENBERG ARCHITECT

ALLAN GREENBERG ARCHITECT

211

RESIDENCES AT CONYERS FARM

Greenwich, Connecticut
1995

STUDIO PEREGALLI

Roberto Peregalli and Laura Sartori Rimini formed the architecture and design firm Studio Peregalli in the early 1990s. Located in Milan, the firm has created entirely new construction and masterful renovations in Europe, the United States, and North Africa. Regardless of the scale of the project, the resulting rooms defy temporal identity thus becoming an essentially timeless setting to frame daily activity. Work develops with deep respect for location, materials, details, and character, based on rigor as well as imagination.

Their point of view on architecture was shaped by Renzo Mongiardino (1916–1998), whom they each had known for different reasons, though both worked with him for more than ten years. During his childhood, Peregalli had met Mongiardino, who was a friend of his parents. He became his pupil and later his partner. Sartori Rimini knew him through a friend who was a client of Mongiardino and she had worked for a while with one of his associates.

Peregalli's academic preparation in philosophy makes him essentially unique among designers, and his fluency in written expression comes to life in his decorative designs. Two books indicate the breadth of his interests as a writer: *The Embroidered Armour* (2008) and *Places and Dust* (2010).[1] The first book explores the relationship between vision and cognition as the basis of Greek thought. The second book is a reflection on contemporary aesthetics. As a student Sartori Rimini focused on the restoration of ancient buildings. From the beginning, she made the focus of her career the relationship between the existing building and its aesthetic renovation, respecting its ancient character while claiming the freedom of new inspiration for the work. In 1991, she opened a studio with Peregalli, where they carried out work of their own while working on other projects associated with Mongiardino until his death.

Laura Sartori Rimini and Roberto Peregalli's approach to architecture is connected to the "nostalgia" of places and the traces it leaves in the surrounding context. The two partners developed working relationships with approximately fifty artisans' firms, which work on their projects all over the world. These range from carpenters, stucco decorators, marble and bronze workers, painters, upholsterers, parquetry layers, and restorers, a team of people able to carry out any work of any dimension starting from scratch. For the architects, the use of salvage materials is fundamental, which they mix with the materials produced by their artisans to create a harmonious whole. Their approach to architecture is thoroughly described in their book *The Invention of the Past: Interior Design and Architecture of Studio Peregalli* (2011). A passage in this book describes the relationship between architecture and memory and its effects on their designs:

> Our idea of place (whether it is a place that we have to build up from nothing or a place that already exists and requires modification) is closely tied to memory and to time. We believe that everything is already there to be seen; therefore we are able to rethink the places and reinvent them. It is the memory— perhaps even with all its imperfections—of a drawing from an old book that comes back to the surface with a haunting echo. Memory of the past should not be conceived as a desire to revive a historical copy, but it should be interpreted as an invention that, arising from the memory of classical forms, is projected toward the future. In a world in which the signature that the artist leaves on the work readily identifies it, our work on the contrary endeavors to blend with its surroundings in an attempt to elude the signature. The highest amount of recognition derives from the assertion that "it would appear that it had always been here."[2]

From architectural spaces to theatrical scenery to the setting of exhibitions and museums, the character of their work can be interpreted as a "reverie" of the past. The fundamental element is the "patina" in which they envelop their environments, and it is a unique expression in current architecture. The patina plunges any object in an aura without time, where memory mixes with invention, creating places of surprising harmony.

VILLA IN ANDALUSIA

Spain
2008

APARTMENT IN MILAN

Italy
1992 (renovation)

APARTMENT IN PARIS

France
2006 (renovation)

HOUSE IN THE MEDINA

Tangier, Morocco
2004 (renovation)

ERNESTO BUCH
ARCHITECT

Founded in 1987 in New Haven, Connecticut, with studios in Miami, Florida, and Punta Cana, Dominican Republic, Ernesto Buch's practice is devoted to classical and traditional architecture and urban design. Buch, who was born in Cuba and raised in Miami, believes his lifelong interest in classical architecture as well as his love of urban life began with the memories of his childhood in Cuba, in particular the vision etched in his mind of Havana, that grand, old, dense, classical city by the sea, juxtaposed with Miami, a relatively young and sprawling metropolis-in-the-making. His training in architecture includes a bachelor of arts degree from Case Western Reserve University, a bachelor of architecture degree from the University of Miami, and a master of architecture degree in urban design from Harvard. His knowledge of classical architecture was strengthened during his time working in the offices of Allan Greenberg. Of this period in his professional life, Ernesto comments, "Working for Allan Greenberg was an education in the finer details of classical and traditional architecture. Besides an architectural practice, Greenberg's office was also a school for classicism, and Allan a great teacher. What I learned there has been invaluable in the development of my work."[1]

A seminal experience earlier in his career involved working with Andrés Duany and Elizabeth Plater-Zyberk as part of the original team that developed the master plan and building code for Seaside, Florida, the vacation community that is considered the beginning of the New Urbanism movement to restore meaningful urban social interaction through sensitive design reflective of place and culture. Buch served as Seaside's second Town Architect, at the end of Teofilo Victoria's term. During this period, Buch designed a number of houses and two small civic buildings. Of these, the Tupelo Street Pavilion, serving as a portal to the beach, soon became the iconic image of Seaside. Describing the character of his architecture, Buch has written:

> As traditionalists, we are committed to an architecture that is responsive to its physical setting. We believe that a building must be an integral part of its surroundings, whether urban or rural. It must be well suited to the climate and respectful of the historical context and the cultural, building, and architectural traditions of the place. We use local building methods and incorporate indigenous materials in our work. We work closely with the builder, artisans, and laborers during the building process. As classicists, we are interested in the language of

classical architecture as manifested through the ages and adapted to various settings, climates, and functions, as well as different social and cultural contexts. We are informed by historical precedents and typologies and are interested in using the local vernacular.[2]

In his firm's early work in Connecticut, focusing on the more formal aspects of classical architecture, Buch put into practice the lessons learned at Greenberg's office on the classical language, the proper use of the orders, and correct detailing. His firm's initial project, a library addition for art historian John Richardson, is a classical pavilion picturesquely placed in a carefully crafted landscape on the grounds of Richardson's country house. This design resulted in his receiving the Arthur Ross Award from Classical America in 1994.

In 1997, Buch traveled to the Dominican Republic to supervise the construction of the seaside vacation house he had designed for Oscar de la Renta, to be built in Punta Cana, a new resort being developed on the island. That initial project led to a number of houses in Punta Cana. Here typologies well suited to this climate were explored, most notably the veranda house, variations of which occur throughout the Caribbean. Buch recalls, "Responding to the climate, all of these houses have extensive covered but open areas for outdoor living in the form of verandas, loggias, and porches, protected from sun and rain, delightful in this warm yet breezy climate of intense sunlight and sudden downpours." Planned for cross ventilation and to take advantage of the ocean breezes, these houses are perfectly comfortable without air-conditioning most of the year.

In all of these houses local materials were used including the beautiful Dominican coral stone, stucco made from crushed, locally quarried limestone, and the colorful cement floor tiles with geometric patterns made popular in parts of Latin America and the Caribbean during the nineteenth century. Classical architecture, introduced by European colonizers and transformed and adapted over the centuries, has a long tradition in these islands. Ernesto's houses have been an exploration of these traditions, exemplified by "La Colina," for interior decorator Bunny Williams and antiques dealer John Rosselli. Evocative of the Southern raised plantation house so beloved by the owners, it is also firmly planted in the tradition of Caribbean English Palladian architecture. Having closely collaborated from the beginning with Williams, Buch feels that "the furnishings and decoration by Williams establish a perfect dialogue with the architecture, both reinforcing each other."

LA COLINA

Corales de Punta Cana, Dominican Republic
2005–2007
Interior Decoration: Bunny Williams

ERNESTO BUCH ARCHITECT

248

DE LA GUARDIA VICTORIA
ARCHITECTS & URBANISTS

In 1988, Teófilo Victoria and Maria de la Guardia founded their firm, first called Office of Architecture and Monumental Art. The current name, De la Guardia Victoria Architects & Urbanists (DLGV), reflects their involvement in the design of both buildings and master plans based on the principles of classical and vernacular architecture and traditional town planning. Of their philosophy they state, "We believe it is the duty of the architect to produce an architecture which, in the words of Alberti, 'gives comfort and the greatest pleasure to mankind, to individual and community alike.'"[1]

Maria de la Guardia received a bachelor of architecture degree from the University of Miami in 1984 and a master of architecture degree from Harvard University in 1986. Teófilo Victoria graduated from the Rhode Island School of Design in 1979 with a bachelor of fine arts and, in 1980, with a bachelor of architecture. In 1982, Victoria completed a master degree in architecture and urban design at Columbia University. The two future partners met while working at the architecture firm Duany Plater-Zyberk on the design of Seaside, the award-winning "new town" in Florida whose design is considered the origin of the movement known as New Urbanism. In 1983, Victoria became the first Town Architect for Seaside.

In addition to his work as a design principal in DLGV, Victoria teaches at the University of Miami, where he has served as the director of the undergraduate program (1995–98) and of the graduate program (1999–2009), and he has been a visiting professor at Cornell University and Harvard University. Maria de la Guardia has also taught at the University of Miami School of Architecture. As professors and thoughtful architects, they have developed a philosophy that directs the design approach of their firm. They have written:

Classical architectural principles, vernacular traditions, folklore and an understanding of contemporary materials and methods of construction contribute to a conception of architecture which is at once reflective and current. As traditionalists, we recognize the unique characteristics of individual sites and localities and appreciate the ability of architecture to define a sense of place and to encourage the well-being and health of our cities and landscapes. We promote working with indigenous materials and local craftsmanship together with innovative technologies to establish meaningful relationships between buildings and their respective physical and cultural context. In our practice design is of equal value to construction, and the same level of craft dedicated to the production of drawings in the studio is applied to the supervision of building at the job site. We encourage close cooperation with owner and builder to ensure that building projects respond fully to the demands of program, budget and a sustainable environment. Regardless of size, every project is a welcomed opportunity, and the completion of buildings is a cause for celebration and a reiteration of our commitment to provide an architecture and urbanism of discernible beauty and civic virtue.[2]

The firm has received numerous awards for their work including the Shutze Award, Palladio Awards, and Congress for the New Urbanism Charter Awards for new buildings as well as numerous awards for their restoration work. The award-winning villa Ca'Liza, rendered in Coralina stone, combines the Italian traditions of Palladio with the British influence on the architecture of the Bahamas. The two partners have also collaborated on projects with Ernesto Buch, another architect met while working at Seaside. Their collaboration produced the exquisite Indian Creek Residence, in Miami, and Eau Chien, in Nassau, both classical designs inspired by the Italian Renaissance and also rendered in local Florida Coralina stone.

CA'LIZA

New Providence, Bahamas
2008
Interior Design: Amanda Lindroth

DE LA GUARDIA VICTORIA ARCHITECTS & URBANISTS

257

EAU CHIEN

The Bahamas, Villa and Pool House
2009
Architecture: DLGV and Ernesto Buch
Interior Design: Amanda Lindroth

DLGV AND ERNESTO BUCH

DLGV AND ERNESTO BUCH

APPLETON & ASSOCIATES

In 1976, Marc Appleton founded the firm of Appleton & Associates, enabling him to pursue a career that did not follow the pattern typical of that period's modernist and postmodernist firms. It was a path that was significantly influenced by the classical and traditional regional architecture of Southern California.

He had spent much of his youth on western ranches, where he "learned haying, riding, roping, hunting, trapping, and fishing . . . ,"[1] experiences which may have fostered an enduring appreciation for regionalism. As an undergraduate he chose not to pursue architecture at Harvard, where Walter Gropius and Josep Lluís Sert had promoted Bauhaus design principles, but instead received a bachelor degree in English literature in 1968. He then received his master of architecture degree from Yale University, where the more liberal influence of postmodernism dominated during the chairmanship of Charles Moore.

In addition to the impact of architects like Moore, Robert Venturi, and James Sterling, the young Yale professor Allan Greenberg opened new avenues of thought. As Appleton says, "Greenberg became perhaps my most enduring influence in that he cultivated the idea that architectural history could be an operative professional resource, not just an interesting field of study. He also introduced us to architects like Edwin Lutyens, Gunnar Asplund, David Adler, McKim, Mead & White, and others, architects who at the time had fallen off almost everyone else's radar."[2]

Through apprenticeships with several firms, including Frank Gehry, Appleton grew uneasy with what he perceived as a primary concern for most architects: "to create innovative and original work that would, by virtue of having a strong personal signature, garner attention and fame." He came to believe "that many architects seemed as selfishly intent on impressing their fellow professionals and competitors as on serving their client's interests."[3] Upon returning to his native California, Appleton tried to promote an architecture that was not so much an original personal statement as a disciplined craft in the service of his clientele. He was intrigued with the concept of architecture as part of a historical continuum rather than as an iconoclastic exercise.

From offices in Santa Monica and Santa Barbara, his firm pursues the planning and design of custom residential, institutional, and commercial projects, but with a regional focus that reflects a significant stylistic diversity. The work includes adaptive reuse and restoration and typically heeds to the credo of one of Appleton's idols, William Wurster, who said in an interview published in *Architectural Record* in 1956, "Architecture is not a goal. Architecture is for life and pleasure and work and for people. The picture frame and not the picture."

That philosophy also led Appleton to devote time to a number of philanthropic causes, and his firm has periodically taken on pro bono projects for nonprofit organizations. He and his family are founding members of the Appleton-Whittel Research Ranch Foundation in Arizona, which is associated with the National Audubon Society in protecting local ecosystems. He also helped found the Mingei International Museum in San Diego, which provides exhibitions and education in art from diverse cultures. He has served on the board of trustees for Prescott College in Arizona, and the Cooper Union and the Institute of Classical Architecture & Art in New York, and he currently serves on the boards for the Lotusland and Casa del Hererro estates in Santa Barbara and the Dean's Council for the Yale School of Architecture.

ZANUCK RESIDENCE

Beverly Hills, California
1989–1991

VILLA CRESTA

Los Angeles, California
1999–2002

MEADOW FARM

Santa Barbara, California
2002–2006

WRITER'S PAVILION

Darien, Connecticut
1998–1999

APPLETON & ASSOCIATES

HISTORICAL CONCEPTS

Historical Concepts was established by James L. Strickland, an Atlanta native who from a young age was captivated by the historic character of the city's neighborhoods. Strickland obtained an undergraduate degree in fine arts from the University of Georgia and then served in the Army Special Forces, but his innate fascination with the South's traditional architecture did not wane. In the early 1970s, the desire to create homes like those he had long admired led him to receive his master of architecture degree from Yale University in 1972.

Through the influence of postmodernism, the field of architecture was enlarging its vision of the possibilities of traditional and classical architecture, but the revival of interest in new classical buildings was yet in its infancy in Atlanta when Strickland founded Historical Concepts as a design-build firm in 1982. Within a few years, the firm's highly detailed traditional designs resulted in growing demand for its architectural services. By the early 1990s, Strickland responded to this trend by refocusing the firm's efforts exclusively on design.

The firm's practice is principally residential, driven by a passion for historic architecture. The early designs for Sweetbottom, a neo-traditional community near Atlanta with homes patterned after those in the historic districts of New Orleans and Savannah, led to commissions in coastal South Carolina and Georgia, where the firm cemented its position as an authority on classic Southern architecture. In these semitropical climates, wood construction and nineteenth-century Greek Revival houses provide the precedents for the firm's new designs, which often have crisp, classically inspired details rendered in simpler fashion than their sources. Reflecting on his response to regional design, Strickland wrote:

> Standing before the fine eighteenth- and nineteenth-century houses of the South and their humble vernacular counterparts, it's impossible not to admire the

thought and love that went into their design and construction. Having evolved in response to specific conditions—climate, cultural traditions, and regional ways of life—they tell us so much about our ancestors and the lives they led.[1]

In the three decades since its inception, Historical Concepts has evolved to comprise a staff of thirty. While Strickland provides leadership as president and senior principal, partners Terry Pylant, Aaron Daily, Andrew Cogar, and Kevin Clark direct design teams composed of graduates from the nation's top traditional architecture programs. Todd Strickland is the managing partner, overseeing the operational aspects of the firm.

Historical Concepts' focus on local vernacular traditions can be found along the East Coast from Jupiter Island, Florida, to the Hamptons and the shores of Maine. The firm's clients have also drawn them westward to the mountains of Montana and Sun Valley, Idaho. In discussing the firm's diverse body of work and ability to adapt to new settings, Strickland has remarked:

> It may sound counterintuitive, but we rarely enter the design process with the idea of faithfully reproducing a specific style. Rather, the natural setting, the region's architecture, and the vision of the client are our guides. As a result, the style in which a house is built evolves gradually in a way that is never forced or unnatural.[2]

The firm's design excellence has been recognized with numerous planning and architecture awards, including Palladio Awards, Shutze Awards, and a Congress for the New Urbanism Charter Award. In 2010, the firm received the Arthur Ross Award for Architecture from the Institute of Classical Architecture & Art in recognition of their significant body of architectural work focusing especially on the vernacular tradition, and in 2012 their work was presented in *Coming Home: The Southern Vernacular House*.

HAMPTON PLANTATION

Riceboro, Georgia
1999–2000

BEAUX ARTS ESTATE

Atlanta, Georgia
2003–2006

SCARBOROUGH FARM

Pine Mountain, Georgia
2008–2010

SERENITY

Bluffton, South Carolina
2006–2009

BOONE RESIDENCE

Spring Island, South Carolina
2004–2005

CRAIG HAMILTON ARCHITECTS

C raig Hamilton is the principal designer of an international practice based in Radnorshire, in Wales. The majority of the firm's projects may be found in the United Kingdom, with some work also in Switzerland and Russia. The work spans new country houses, chapels, extensions to historic buildings, and commercial and urban designs including an extension to the historic town of Penrith in Cumbria that included two town squares and numerous associated buildings.

Hamilton is philosophically dedicated to a modern classical architecture informed by a broad and deep understanding of the classical tradition. Commenting on Hamilton's approach to design, Gavin Stamp has written:

> In the superficial, polarized debate about architecture today, Hamilton would have to be labeled as a "traditionalist" as he is one of those who believes that something useful and beautiful can still be said in the language of the Greeks and Romans. But, unlike many in his camp, he is not in thrall to the cult of Palladio . . . Hamilton is so much wider and more intelligent in his outlook, for he is acutely aware of so many more architects in the past who have demonstrated how it is possible to be expressive, original and, yes, truly modern in Classical terms.[1]

Hamilton finds great appeal in the work of an array of classical architects who reinterpreted accepted traditions including Ictinus, architect of the Parthenon during the fifth century BCE; Karl Friedrich Schinkel, a nineteenth-century Prussian architect; and C. R. Cockerell, a nineteenth-century British architect. He views his work as a direct continuation of the twentieth-century classical tradition in Great Britain created by architects Charles Holden, Sir Edwin Lutyens, Giles Gilbert Scott, E. Vincent Harris, and the firm of Burnet, Tait & Lorne.

Although trained in a modernist program of architecture at the University of Natal in Durban, South Africa, he was influenced by Professor Barrie

Biermann, described by Hamilton as "an exceptional scholar, architect, and draughtsman who taught the history of architecture as a design tool."[2] Although a modernist himself, Biermann taught the orders and instilled a deep love of the ancient classical world. From Biermann, Hamilton learned the discipline of keeping sketchbooks and recording and measuring buildings, as well as the importance of hand drawing. Hamilton further developed his abilities as a classicist through dedicated study and countless journeys within the United Kingdom and abroad to view, measure, and draw buildings that inspired him.

In 1985, Hamilton relocated to the United Kingdom and apprenticed with architect Michael Reardon in Warwickshire, where he worked on "The Other Place" theater for the Royal Shakespeare Company among other projects. In 1991, Hamilton established an architectural practice focused on new classical buildings and new buildings in the context of historic structures.

Two of Hamilton's most impressive monumental buildings are a private Catholic chapel in the north of Britain and a pool pavilion located on the grounds of a historic country house in Gloucestershire designed by Sir John Soane. Both buildings demonstrate the architect's belief in the integration of architecture and sculpture, and Hamilton adheres to C. R. Cockerell's statement that sculpture is the "voice of architecture." On both the chapel and pool pavilion, Hamilton worked closely with Alexander Stoddart, Sculptor in Ordinary to The Queen in Scotland, to integrate symbolically eloquent sculpture into the design. In 2006, the chapel received the Georgian Group Award for the best new building in the classical tradition. Hamilton also believes in the continuation of the tradition of hand drawing in the process of the making of architecture. He is a distinguished draughtsman and watercolorist, and his work is exhibited regularly in London.

PRIVATE CATHOLIC CHAPEL

North of Britain
2005

WILLIAMSTRIP POOL PAVILION

Gloucestershire, England
2012

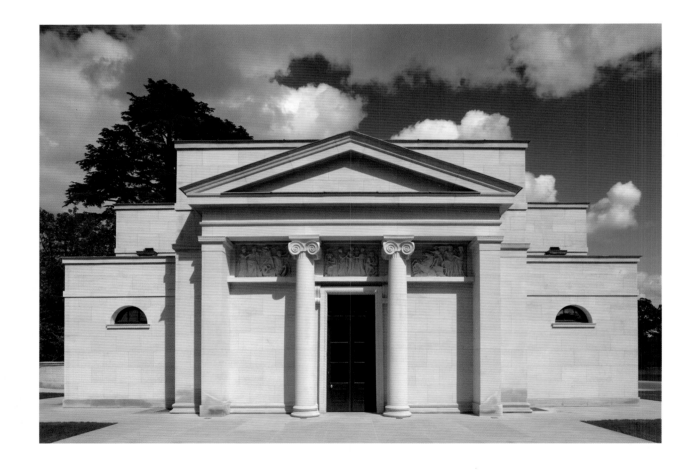

WILLIAMSTRIP PARK

New Entrance and East Wing
Gloucestershire, England
2010

COED MAWR FARM

Radnorshire, Wales
2007

UPTON HOUSE

Gloucestershire, England
2005

J. P. MOLYNEUX STUDIO

Juan Pablo Molyneux heads an international interior design firm with offices in New York City and Paris. A native of Santiago, Chile he studied architecture at the Pontificia Universidad Católica de Chile, and the Ecole des Beaux-arts and the Ecole du Louvre in Paris. Of his education in Chile, he recalls, "We studied absolutely nothing classical at all. It was as if the history of architecture began with the twentieth century. We were pushed very much toward engineering, a socially conscious approach that was very typical of the period."[1] He attended the schools in Paris to acquire training he was not receiving in Chile and found inspiration in the work of Jacques-Ange Gabriel, Andrea Palladio, and Graeco-Roman architecture in general. Following his earliest work, he transitioned from the modernism of his school years to become a thoroughly committed classicist. His biographer Michael Frank described this transition:

> Juan Pablo Molyneux was not born the full-fledged designer of the urbane, polished, and often neoclassical interiors for which he is best known. [His] architecturally confident rooms . . . are the product of a lifetime of study, observation, and a good deal of trial and error. Like many journeys of creative development, Molyneux's has been accompanied by its share of fits and starts, but he has been careful to learn even from the early influences he later chose to react against. The versatility of Molyneux's present design vocabulary owes a good deal to his coming of age in the aesthetically strict world of modernism and then opening himself up to the more historically oriented realm of neoclassicism. It is in this combination that he has found his most suitable, his most comfortable, home.[2]

After graduation from college, he opened his first design office in Santiago, Chile, and, in 1975, opened an office in Buenos Aires, Argentina, where he designed significant interior renovations of many opulent nineteenth-century buildings. In 1982, he relocated his headquarters to New York City after deciding that this city offered him a wider range of design resources and an exciting professional milieu. Throughout his career, he maintained his allegiance to Paris and in 1998 opened a branch office in the heart of historic Paris. From these two offices, Molyneux produces work throughout the United States and Europe, in Russia, Canada, and South America, as well as the Middle East. His work includes interior design of corporate headquarters, a range of residential work from individual apartments to a seven-story town house, the restoration of historic buildings including a Beaux-Arts apartment in Buenos Aires and a seventeenth-century *hôtel particulier* in Paris, as well as the interior of a Boeing 737 and several suites aboard the ocean liner *World of Residensea*. Among his exceptional public projects are the winning competition design of the Pavilion of Treaties at the Konstantinovsky Palace, St. Petersburg, Russia, and renovation and interior design of the main banquet room and reception salon at the Cercle de L' Union Interalliée, in Paris.

His firm's work has been recognized by numerous professional publications as well as inclusion in nineteen books. Molyneux joined a list of influential figures in design and the performing arts when he received the Decoration of the Chevalier des Arts et Lettres. In 2004, the French Minister of Culture gave him this award to acknowledge his assistance in spreading French culture through his design work and his support of artisans. He is a member of the boards of directors of The World Monuments Fund in Europe, The French Heritage Society and the American Friends of Versailles.

UPPER EAST SIDE
TOWN HOUSE

New York, New York

J. P. MOLYNEUX STUDIO

HÔTEL PARTICULIER CLAUDE PASSART

Paris, France
2004–2012

J. P. MOLYNEUX STUDIO

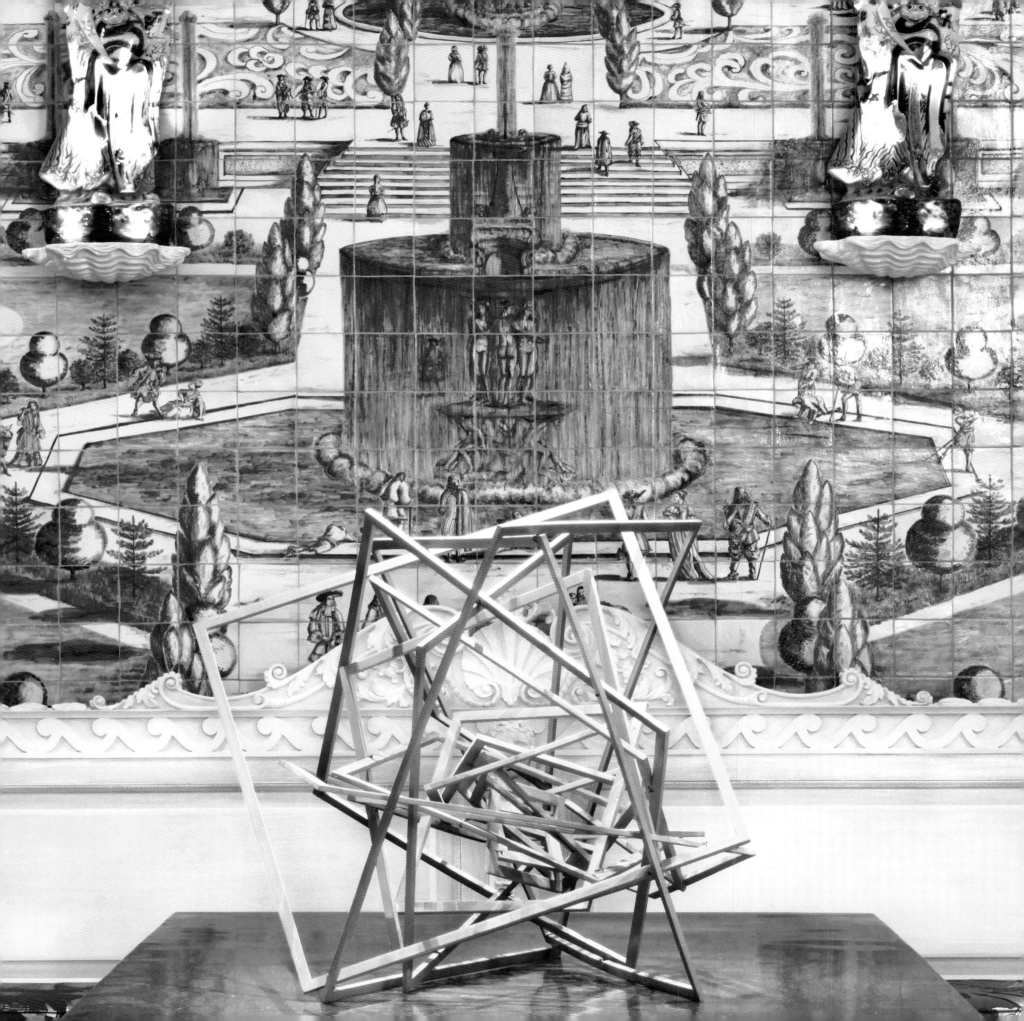

J. P. MOLYNEUX STUDIO

J. P. MOLYNEUX STUDIO

CHÂTEAU DU MARAIS

Val-Saint-Germain, France
2006

QUINLAN & FRANCIS TERRY ARCHITECTS

The firm of Quinlan & Francis Terry Architects extends the lineage of classical design from the firm of Erith & Terry, which operated from 1968 to 2003. Quinlan Terry was born and brought up in the heart of the modernist movement: his parents were friends with Walter Gropius, Brutalist architect Erno Goldfinger, and abstract sculptor Barbara Hepworth, and in high school his greatest interest was sculpture. During his years at the Architecture Association, from 1955 to 1961, he became increasingly disillusioned with modernism and longed for more traditional, classical, and stable design principles. Upon graduation, Quinlan's dissatisfaction with current design inspired him to work with Raymond Erith (1904–1973), the most respected traditional designer in Britain at that time.

Quinlan Terry's son, Francis, spent much of his childhood accompanying his father on sketching trips, and his vacations from college were often spent working in his father's office. He received his architectural training at Cambridge University. After graduation he worked as an apprentice with Allan Greenberg and for a period explored a career as an artist. After a short time he realized the benefit of combining his interests in art and architecture. With his talent in figurative art, Francis designs the firm's imaginative sculptural decoration, an essential element in the continued vitality of the classical tradition.

Father and son share a philosophy emphasizing traditional materials, construction methods, and symbolic ornament as valuable solutions for modern architecture, but they have found, albeit infrequently, that a given budget may demand some nontraditional detailing. Their preferred material choices are not made merely to evoke an historic appearance, but also to express the ethical integrity that characterizes their work. For every project, the firm demonstrates the financial viability of traditional construction and traditional methods of lighting and ventilation when considered through the lifetime of the building. Such concepts are in line with the most current environmentally conscious architects. In addition, their work has demonstrated that solutions for modern problems can be accomplished through traditional design. In a 1987 speech for the Oxford Union debate, Quinlan argued, "We cannot think seriously of architecture without raising at the same time the fundamental question of man's life on earth . . . let us build smaller and gentler buildings; let us make walls of solid brick or stone; let us roof them with slates and pierce them with sash windows of the kind that have recommended themselves to generations of Englishmen; let us use the Doric, Ionic and Corinthian Orders; and let us take inspiration from the wisdom of our forefathers, so that our buildings will be signs and heralds of a more natural, more stable and more beautiful world."[1]

The firm's work includes mid-rise office buildings, multiuse complexes, churches, theaters, libraries, and numerous country houses in England, Germany, and the United States. The firm also restored and added new details to the three state rooms at No. 10 Downing Street. Their work has received numerous awards including the Royal Fine Arts Commission's Building of the Year Award for Downing College Library in 1994; the Philippe Rotthier European Prize for the Reconstruction of the City in 1982 and 2008; and the Georgian Group's 2003, 2008, and 2009 Best New Building in the Classical Tradition Award, for Ferne Park, Ferne Park Summerhouse, and the office building at 264–267 Tottenham Court Road. Quinlan Terry's work has been recognized by the two most significant career awards in classical design: the Arthur Ross Award for Architecture, in 2002, and the Richard H. Driehaus Prize for Classical Architecture, in 2005. Francis Terry's exquisite drawings are regularly exhibited at the Royal Academy in London, and he received the Worshipful Company of Chartered Architects' prize for architectural drawing in 2002. Quinlan and Francis Terry have created buildings whose excellence assures their place among the masters of British architecture.

HANOVER LODGE

Regents Park
London, England
2002–2009

QUINLAN & FRANCIS TERRY ARCHITECTS

373

QUINLAN & FRANCIS TERRY ARCHITECTS

QUINLAN & FRANCIS TERRY ARCHITECTS

376

QUINLAN & FRANCIS TERRY ARCHITECTS

377

QUINLAN & FRANCIS TERRY ARCHITECTS

380

JULIAN BICKNELL
& ASSOCIATES

Julian Bicknell's London-based firm is dedicated to the design of exquisitely detailed public and private buildings. His architecture is both pragmatic and theatrical. His houses seek to combine a practical and contemporary approach to modern domestic life with the elegance of traditional design, and to combine the advantages of modern technology and mass-production with occasions for pleasure, surprise, and fine craftsmanship. His larger buildings are formal but at the same time playful. He relishes the combination and contrast of different styles, and his work has ranged from high Gothic through half-timbered Elizabethan, Baroque, Neoclassical, and Victorian, to the plate glass and polished metal of the present day. His designs are often based on rigorous geometric systems designed in the first instance to order and simplify the process of construction but which have, as a by-product, the calm inevitability of classical architecture and interiors. He frequently employs illusions of scale and a sense of theatrical progression through his buildings. Most of his work is in Britain and Japan, but he has undertaken projects all over the world including the United States, Germany, France, Russia, and Kazakhstan.

Bicknell studied at Cambridge University both as an undergraduate and graduate student. Prior to setting up his own firm in 1983, Bicknell worked first for Ted Cullinan, then as director of the Project Office at the Royal College of Art, and lastly for Arup Associates, the architectural branch of the multinational engineering firm. He was a founding trustee of the Prince of Wales's Institute of Architecture (now the Prince's Foundation for Building Community) and served on the faculty there from 1990 to 2000 as well as teaching at the Institute's summer schools in Italy, Germany, France, and the United Kingdom.

Bicknell began his career deploying a modern vernacular in work on existing buildings. His first overtly classical work was his design in 1978 for the new Garden Hall at Castle Howard in Yorkshire, a location for scenes in the television adaptation of *Brideshead Revisited*. There followed his first full-scale classical building, at Henbury Rotonda, Cheshire (1983), a design developed from a *capriccio* by the painter Felix Kelly commissioned by Sebastian de Ferranti. Explaining subtle aspects of the realized house, Bicknell remarked:

> The design belongs to a British lineage of English Neo-Palladian in the Vanbrugh manner. I have little sympathy or enthusiasm for Burlington's unoriginal dogma. I believe he successfully extinguished the tradition of creative architectural thinking fostered by Wren in the generation of Hawksmoor, Vanbrugh, Gibbs, and Archer—a creative tradition that didn't recover until Dance and Soane a hundred years later.[1]

Describing his own work, Bicknell has written, "Whether built or not, each design is the culmination of a long and sometimes tortuous process of evolution, the result of repeated trial and error, of careful consultation, second thoughts and reversions to earlier ideas. Each is a creative exercise; each a learning process; each contributes to the store of knowledge and experience—on which subsequent designs may draw."[2]

Bicknell draws inspiration from early eighteenth-century Baroque and Palladian architecture. On many projects he has worked closely with the noted carver Dick Reid to create fine decorative design features like the figurative carving in the fireplace surround for a historic house in Dorset. Reid retired in 2004 and will be remembered for his restoration carving for Spencer House and Windsor Castle (fig. 2.14). In his formal interiors, Bicknell seizes the theatrical opportunities offered by the elaborate carving and deeply modeled plasterwork of the early eighteenth century, enhancing his rooms with a stately ebullience and borrowed grandeur that draws those who use them into a more imaginative world.

CASTLE HOWARD

Garden Hall and Library
Yorkshire, England
1980–1983

CARDEN HALL

Cheshire, England
2001–2004

JULIAN BICKNELL & ASSOCIATES

HENBURY HALL

Cheshire, England
1984–1986

JULIAN BICKNELL & ASSOCIATES

ROYAL CREST HOUSE

Takasaki, Japan
2002–2004

CRANBORNE MANOR

Dorset, England
2000

FOREST OF BERE

Hampshire, England
2007–2010

JULIAN BICKNELL & ASSOCIATES

400

JOHN SIMPSON
& PARTNERS

John Simpson is one of the most active proponents of classical and traditional architecture in Britain, specializing in new construction and restoration of public and private buildings as well as interior and furniture design. He is a second-generation traditional architect, one of the few current classicists able to claim such a heritage—his father received classical training in architecture and designed traditional styled buildings before World War II. When the younger Simpson attended the Bartlett School of Architecture and Planning at the University of London beginning in 1972, his education was modernist tempered with postmodern acceptance of the potential enrichment of history. In 1975, while working for Duffy, Eley, Giffoni, and Worthington, Simpson catalogued and surveyed buildings in Covent Garden and he attributes his interest in historic architecture to the lessons learned in this study. Of this experience he has said, "The conclusion to which I had come was that architecture was essentially a language for the art of building. As with any language, it was necessary to understand its intricacies and the canon of work associated with it, before you could produce lasting and significant works."[1]

After receiving his postgraduate diploma from Bartlett, he pursued his own self-education in traditional architecture by studying the work of John Soane and eighteenth- and early nineteenth-century buildings. Of this period he says, "I traveled to study and measure a number of [Soane's] surviving buildings to which I could gain access. Invariably, I was amazed at how much Soane always managed to pack into one space, for when I measured I found that the dimensions were always smaller than I expected, despite their monumentality. Also, discovering the tricks he used to create apparent symmetry out of such irregular shapes, I found especially instructive the way in which he fitted new rooms within the constraints of existing buildings."[2] Finally prepared for a career in traditional and classical architecture, Simpson established his own firm in 1980, which focuses on public and private buildings and master planning.

Simpson's public architecture displays his eclectic approach, which combines disparate works into intriguingly evocative forms and spaces. Among his most significant public works, the Queen's Gallery at Buckingham Palace and Gonville and Caius College at Cambridge University combine classical Greek details with the more recent inspiration of John Soane. Always based on programmatic references, his stylistic choices are not arbitrary. For example, at Cambridge he drew inspiration for a new Fellows' Dining Hall from the cella of the Temple of Apollo Epicurius at Bassae, in homage to C. R. Cockerell, the English architect whose research of Bassae is housed in Cambridge in a brilliant display of the adaptability and inclusiveness of the classical language of architecture (fig. 6.6). In 2012, Simpson replanned the circulation around Kensington Palace and created a new entrance and a new extension to provide visitor facilities. The new entrance loggia was designed to celebrate the Diamond Jubilee of Queen Elizabeth II in its decorative ornament.

Simpson's individual buildings and urban planning schemes have received recognition in his native Britain as well as in Belgium and the United States. The Georgian Group awarded his firm the prize for Best New Classical Building in 2003 for the Queen's Gallery and in 2010 for the Pipe Partridge Building for Lady Margaret Hall, at Oxford University. His master plan for Fairford Leys, near Aylesbury, received the Philippe Rotthier European Prize for Architecture in 2008; the Palladio Award for Architecture in 2007 was given to the Carhart Mansion in New York City; and in 2008 Simpson was given the Arthur Ross Award in recognition of his lifetime achievement in architecture.

QUEEN'S GALLERY

Buckingham Palace
London, England
2002

JOHN SIMPSON & PARTNERS

404

GONVILLE AND CAIUS COLLEGE

Cambridge, England
1995

KENSINGTON PALACE MASTER PLAN

London, England
2012

FAIRFAX & SAMMONS ARCHITECTS

Both Anne Fairfax and Richard Sammons received their professional architectural education at the University of Virginia and, after graduation, sought education in classical design through apprenticeship—Sammons, the firm's design director, first worked in Manhattan for David Anthony Easton, a classicist specializing in residential design, and Fairfax worked in Virgina for John Paul Hanbury, who was known for his finely crafted Tidewater Virginia regional architecture. In Easton's office, Sammons learned detailing from Joe Marino, who in his eighties conveyed the practical knowledge learned in the firm of Cross and Cross Architects, a prominent New York firm best remembered for their Art Deco skyscrapers. After her time in Hanbury's office, Fairfax returned to her native Honolulu, where she designed classical vernacular residences inspired by the local work in Hawaii of Bertram Goodhue, David Adler, and Charles W. Dickey.

In 1992, the two established their partnership devoted to the design of exquisitely detailed residences. Their offices in Manhattan and Palm Beach now offer design services in architecture, interior decoration, and urban design. Of their work Sammons has said, "We intentionally have no signature style . . . we tailor everything to the setting, the climate, the owner's temperament. The work is about restraint, scale and proportion, not about calling attention to ourselves. We refine and refine the details to the utmost level possible, and always with an armature of proportional logic. In our work there are no arbitrary moves."[1]

Fairfax and Sammons employ the classicist's methodology of design—research of the most fitting precedents precedes abstract conception of design. Examples are an image for a classical seaside residence developed from such wide-ranging historical roots as the Charleston single house type, the climatically responsive tropical British Colonial architecture, and the geometrically complex rooms of Thomas Jefferson. These enormously varied sources resulted in a newly conceived residential solution appropriate to the Florida climate, landscape, and ocean vistas.

The firm's philosophy demands careful attention to room proportion and detailing. Sammons and Fairfax have both shared their knowledge of these subjects as visiting professors and jurists at the Georgia Institute of Technology, the University of Notre Dame, the University of Miami, and Yale University, and in continuing education classes offered by the Institute of Classical Architecture and Art. They are devoted to expanding the availability of information formerly known by all architects but lost through the dominance of modernist theory in architectural education. For example, Sammons provided an illustrated foreword to the reissued 1926 *Theory of Mouldings* by C. Howard Walker so that current designers could understand a subject so basic that its terminology needed no introduction in the original text.

The emergence of classical and traditional design as a major movement in twenty-first-century America is due in large measure to the dedicated partnership of Anne Fairfax and Richard Sammons. Sammons was a founding director of the Institute of Classical Architecture and Art (ICA&A) and, in 1991, an instructor at the Prince of Wales Institute in Britain. The firm's office also provided headquarters for Henry Hope Reid's Classical America, the sole organization challenging modernist aesthetics until the establishment of the ICA&A in 1992. Fairfax served as the chairman of the board of the Institute of Classical Architecture and Art as well as a trustee for the Royal Oak Foundation, and, along with Sammons, is one of thirty-nine elected members of the College of Practitioners of the International Network for Traditional Building, Architecture & Urbanism (INTBAU). Their architectural and urban design work has received numerous awards and has been the subject of the monograph *American Houses: The Architecture of Fairfax & Sammons*. Their work was recognized with the 2013 Arthur Ross Award for Architecture.

A CITY APARTMENT

Park Avenue
New York, New York
1996

A PALM BEACH ESTATE

South Ocean Boulevard
Palm Beach, Florida
2000

GEORGIAN REVIVAL HOUSE

Lexington, Kentucky
2009

NEW GEORGIAN RESIDENCE

Washington, Connecticut
1997

DAVID JONES ARCHITECTS

In 1990, David Jones founded his firm in Washington, D.C., with the idea of designing uncompromising houses based on the history and culture of classical Washington and neighboring Virginia and Maryland. Jones came to this ideal through a challenging academic and professional apprenticeship and early career, at a time when architects were exploring different ways of integrating modern design with the local and regional traditions of American cities, towns, and landscapes. Jones studied at Princeton University during the 1960s, where he received both his undergraduate and graduate architectural degrees. At a time when minimalist modernism reigned, Princeton—with studio masters such as Michael Graves and Richard Meier—remained focused on the past. Many hours were spent analyzing the early work of Le Corbusier and other International Style architects for an understanding of their systems of proportions, their compositions, and the ideas that guided their process. This analysis then informed the student's own design work. To better understand the architectural ideas of other eras, Jones eagerly took all the architecture history courses Princeton offered. He spent one of his graduate school years at Cambridge University, traveling through Europe on breaks.

Following service in the Peace Corps and Navy, he joined Hartman-Cox Architects, then a fledgling firm in Washington just gaining a national reputation for single-family houses as well as large commercial buildings. There he found colleagues who shared similar academic experiences and interests. Principals trained at Princeton and Yale had attracted others who coupled expertise in modern design with a keen intellectual exploration of history and tradition. As Hartman-Cox gradually moved from multilayered, contextual modernism to buildings more straightforwardly based on Washington's context of history and classicism, Jones left to follow his own somewhat parallel path.

Partnering with fellow Princeton graduate and Hartman-Cox alumnus Guy Martin, he formed Martin & Jones Architects in 1977. They earned a reputation for their early postmodern commercial and multifamily residential buildings, garnering awards and entries in guides to the architecture of Washington. Over the next decade, Jones's work shifted from mannerist postmodern buildings to more readily understood, historically "correct" classical and regional vernacular compositions. Jones ultimately found he preferred designing custom homes, where the architect-client relationship is more personal.

He moved once again to create a practice based on high-quality, traditionally inspired houses—a bold but logical step. While David Jones Architects remains focused on the Mid-Atlantic region, the firm has completed houses all along the East Coast. "One advantage of working with traditional models is that other design firms and craftspeople are often better able to understand a project's 'language' and adjust their work to fit the whole," says Jones.[1] Far from inhibiting creativity, Jones believes historical precedent can free team members to create variations on a mutually accepted theme. While the firm has a list of favorite collaborators, the location of a house and the owner's own network often suggest a locally assembled team, usually coordinated by Jones and is staff.

David Jones Architects emphasizes the holistic nature of its projects in its awards submissions, which Jones thinks is a factor in the firm's wide range of awards. American Institute of Architects design juries throughout the region honor the firm's work alongside more numerous modernist winners, citing its fine detailing and regional appropriateness. Among tradition-oriented prizes, the firm has been recognized with Shutze Awards by the Southeast Chapter of the Institute of Classical Architecture and Art, and has won three national Palladio Awards for Best New Traditional House given by *Period Homes* magazine.

SCOTTISH GEORGIAN

Potomac, Maryland
2002

TALL OAKS

McLean, Virginia
2000

RIVERFRONT

Washington, D.C.
2005

DAVID JONES ARCHITECTS

440

DAVID JONES ARCHITECTS

442

G. P. SCHAFER ARCHITECT

In 2002, Gil Schafer followed in the family tradition of his grandfather and great-great-grandfather and established an architectural practice in which he has specialized in residential design. His family background inspired a love of older houses that influenced the focus of his career and the stylistic direction of his firm. Of his youth, Schafer has written, "Over the course of my childhood, I was fortunate to be exposed to life in a variety of places, including the Midwest, Northeast, Georgia, California, and the Bahamas, each contributing to my sense of what makes places unique and how architectural traditions and lifestyle are influenced by context."[1]

Schafer received his undergraduate education with a focus on the growth and structure of cities at Haverford College and its sister institution, Bryn Mawr, both colleges located in the suburbs of Philadelphia. For his architectural training, Schafer attended the Yale School of Architecture and received a master's degree in 1988. While at Yale, Schafer studied under noted practitioners Thomas Beeby, Robert Venturi, Josef Kleihues, Frank Gehry, and Benard Tschumi, who presented a variety of philosophies of modern and postmodern architecture. In his final semester, he was awarded the H. I. Feldman Prize, Yale's highest honor for studio work. After briefly working for Tschumi, he shifted away from a modernist direction to the kind of architecture that had drawn him to the profession in the first place, working at several outstanding classical residential firms including Robert Orr & Associates, Peter Pennoyer Architects, and Ferguson Murray & Shamamian Architects.

In establishing his own practice, Schafer has rooted his firm's work in the historic American classical and vernacular traditions that he has loved since childhood while adapting those traditions to the realities of contemporary lifestyles. "We love the character, detail, and scale of old houses," he says, "but we also love the way that they impart a sense of home."[2] Gil strongly believes that a new-old house can be as livable today as any contemporary one.

In developing their carefully crafted designs, the firm explores "imperfection" and the manner in which the concept can shape their work using historic styles. With respect to this aspect of their work, Schafer explains:

> The more I spent time looking at American vernacular and classical houses, the more I realized that they weren't always perfectly "correct" in terms of what the classical canon might dictate. Sometimes proportions were adjusted—elongated or made more squat—to fit the parameters of a location or to convey a sense of lightness, or weight. Sometimes details were left out; sometimes molding shapes were simplified as determined by the abilities of the amateur builder who made them.[3]

These ideas can be detected in the projects that follow: Greek Revival details mixing with Federal; odd placement of a door or window, sometimes slightly off axis; and very subtle use of moldings in purposefully unresolved manners.

In addition to his architectural practice, Schafer lectures on the relevance and livability of traditional residential architecture today and also serves on several nonprofit boards. From 1999 to 2006, Schafer served as the president and then chairman of the Institute of Classical Architecture & Classical America, now called the Institute of Classical Architecture & Art, and continues to serve as a trustee.

LONGFIELD FARM

Middlefield, New York
2007

G. P. SCHAFER ARCHITECT

A GREEK REVIVAL HOUSE

Millbrook, New York
2007

WILLOW GRACE FARM

Dover Plains, New York
2007

FERGUSON & SHAMAMIAN ARCHITECTS

Mark Ferguson and Oscar Shamamian founded their firm in 1988 on a shared enthusiasm for the formal classical and regional traditional details that characterize the firm's work, and on a desire to achieve a creative synthesis of historical style, regional character, and personal taste with every project. They believe the past offers guidance and inspiration for making and sustaining humane and beautiful environments, and that good design survives the test of time. Their approach dicates that the past not be copied but rather interpreted to adapt to the client and to circumstance. Incremental change is favored over radical change to minimize the disruption to places and to encourage continuity without discouraging innovation.

Both partners received modern educations—Ferguson at Princeton and Shamamian at Columbia—but the period of their training, in the early 1980s, was shaped by the more philosophically open period of postmodernism. Although classical design was actively discouraged in school, Ferguson recalls:

> Oscar Shamamian and I studied architecture when progressive designs by prominent architects turned away from machine-age, cubistic forms in favor of historical forms. They turned away from building based on steel, concrete, glass, and air conditioning in favor of beaux arts planning, a way of designing based on traditional masonry and wood buildings. Thick walls, high ceilings, rooms, windows, doors, hierarchies of privacy and embellishment, are the hallmark of a traditional plan and together they establish an order based on simple things that make buildings legible, like front and back, and top and bottom.[1]

The detailed knowledge Ferguson needed to create excellent classical and traditional design was, by necessity, self-taught. He launched his personal education with the study of *The American Vignola*, by William R. Ware, and, for details, consulted the *Fragments d'architecture antique* by Hector d'Espouy and the *Edifices de Rome moderne* by Paul Letarouilly.

Shamamian first discovered his interest in classical design while working part-time as a photo researcher for Robert A. M. Stern's book project

New York 1900. While gathering the images of projects by turn-of-the-century American classical architects such as McKim, Mead & White and Delano & Aldrich, he discovered a profound fascination that modern design had failed to inspire. He was additionally inspired by his surroundings at Columbia, whose campus plan and notable Low Library had been designed by McKim, Mead & White. He brought this new interest in historical reference to his studio projects, but found no support for them in the milieu of the Columbia graduate studio. The lack of tolerance for historical design was particularly surprising considering the historic campus that surrounded the architecture students as well as the university's celebrated Avery Library, the most significant architectural collection in America. Like Ferguson, Shamamian found that he would have to teach himself in order to develop his understanding of traditional and classical architecture. However, he did find support for his interests in art and architecture history courses and in the office of Stern, a sympathetic mentor. Ferguson and Shamamian met at the renowned interior design firm of Parish-Hadley Associates, which assisted Jacqueline Kennedy in the decoration of the White House and also with the personal residences of the president and his wife, and where both Ferguson and Shamamian had their first classical and traditional design opportunities, in the early 1980s—Ferguson with an addition to a small fieldstone cottage originally designed by Ernest Flagg, and Shamamian with the renovation of a 1920s Georgian mansion in Washington, D.C.

Their fifty-person firm, located in New York City, has completed projects throughout the United States. The firm's core practice is the design of custom residences, including city apartments, suburban houses, and country estates. Their work is characterized by a relationship with local building traditions, landscape, and regional environment, and a passion for excellent detailing, use of fine materials, and exceptional workmanship. Their holistic vision of design has led to notable collaborations with a number of the country's top decorators, landscape architects, artisans, and builders, for which the firm is highly regarded in the industry and has received numerous awards including the 2003 Arthur Ross Award.

HOUSE IN BRIDGEWATER

Bridgewater, Connecticut
1993

HOUSE IN CHAGRIN FALLS

Chagrin Falls, Ohio
2005

AN APARTMENT IN NEW YORK

New York
1998

HOUSE IN WESTPORT

Westport, Connecticut
2008

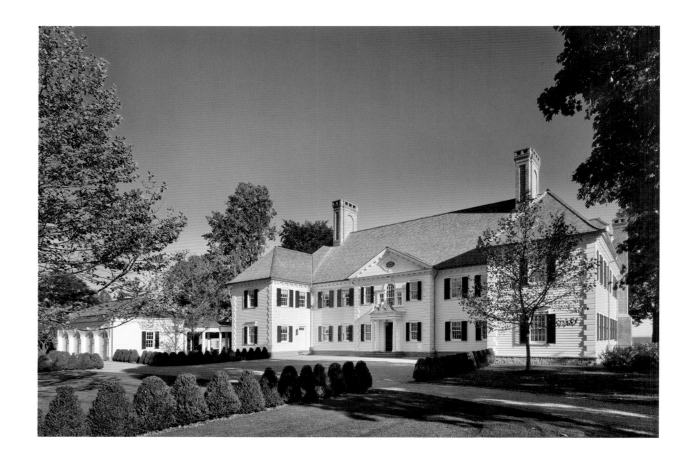

ROBERT A. M. STERN ARCHITECTS

One of the world's leading architects, Robert A. M. Stern enjoys a professional recognition that stems from his numerous activities as an architect, writer, teacher, and lecturer. In 1986, his humor and insight reached a vast audience through his eight-hour documentary television series on the Public Broadcasting System titled *Pride of Place: Building the American Dream*, which brought into America's living rooms a new understanding and respect for architecture.

Stern received his master's degree in architecture from Yale University in 1965 and opened his first practice in 1969, and he continues to direct the design of each project produced by his 150-person firm. Along with Michael Graves and Robert Venturi, Stern initiated the postmodernism movement, which opened a dialogue around the fundamental place of history in an architect's education and, consequently, in the practice of architecture. Although Venturi and Graves each worked to increase the expressive quality of modern architecture, only Stern allowed his work to explore the noncanonical realm of historic inspiration. Stern's firm does not have a single stylistic expression but draws forth an appropriate expression from the needs and context of each program. Stern states:

> I am not interested in a personal style or being part of a singular stylistic movement. I am interested in the suggestive possibilities of the place. I want my buildings to be portraits of the places where they are built. For this reason I am less interested in architecture as the representation of innovative genius and more interested in architecture as the act of contextual invention.[1]

Over the course of his long career Stern has demonstrated the richness of an eclectic approach to design. His willingness to explore historic sources brings greater meaning to architecture through connections of the present with the past. His continuing interest in the Shingle Style derives from its appropriateness as an American form balancing rough texture with refined massing and detail. His acknowledgment that public architecture demands an expressive scale, order, and symbolism enriches such buildings as libraries and museums with the readable ornament that reminds the citizenry of their heritage. In his many "goodtime places" produced for The Walt Disney Company, he draws upon the expressive power of humor.

Stern has served as teacher and mentor for students at Columbia and Yale and has inspired scores of other students and professionals through the example of his work. From 1984 to 1988, he was the first director of Columbia's Temple Hoyne Buell Center for the Study of American Architecture. In 1998, he was named dean of the Yale School of Architecture. Unlike the vast majority of American architecture programs, Stern has presented students with the full array of eclectic philosophies of current design including leading proponents of classical and traditional architecture. He has broadened the understanding of American architecture through the numerous books that he has authored or coauthored, translations of which have been published in Spanish, Italian, and Japanese; fifteen monographs on the work of his firm have been published. His 1975 biography of George Howe was an early exploration of a traditional architect whose later work produced an American face for the International Style. Stern's career mirrored Howe's, but in reverse. As Stern matured in thinking and experience, his work displayed an increasingly diverse and poetic production moving away from the earlier simple abstractions that marked his youthful creations.

The firm of Robert A. M. Stern Architects has received numerous design awards, and Stern's personal contributions to architecture have been recognized with major awards including the 2011 Richard H. Driehaus Prize for Classical Architecture; in 2008, he received the tenth Vincent Scully Prize from the National Building Museum; in 2007, he received both the Athena Award from the Congress for the New Urbanism and the Board of Directors' Honor from the Institute of Classical Architecture and Classical America.

FIFTEEN CENTRAL PARK WEST

New York, New York
2008

ROBERT A. M. STERN ARCHITECTS

HOUSE AT SEASIDE

Seaside, Florida
2006

NASHVILLE PUBLIC LIBRARY

Nashville, Tennessee
2001

ROBERT A. M. STERN ARCHITECTS

480

CHAPTER SIX

ORNAMENT

A Source of Beauty

DAVID WATKIN

[6.1] *James Stuart and Nicholas Revett,*
Antiquities of Athens, Supplement, vol. V
(1830), "Interior Order of the Cella of the
Temple of Jupiter Olympius, at Agrigentum,"
pl. VI. Also published in C. R. Cockerell,
The Temple of Jupiter Olympius at Agrigentum
(1830), pl. VI.

[6.2] *Corinthian order capital, "from different sites in Rome," with entablature and figured frieze.* Vignola, Canon of the Five Orders of Architecture *(1562, etc.), pl. 26*

[6.3 OPPOSITE] *"Regular Mouldings with Their Proper Ornaments," plate from William Chambers,* Treatise on the Decorative Part of Civil Architecture *(1791).*

THE THEORETICAL BACKGROUND

It is important to be aware that in classical architecture and the associated interior design, the role played by the orders, Tuscan, Doric, Ionic, Corinthian, and Composite, is itself largely ornamental (fig. 6.2). This was clearly established by Giacomo Barozzi da Vignola (1507–1573) in his fundamental source book, *Regola delli cinque ordini d'architettura* (1562), where he explained in his account of the Tuscan order that, "having failed to find in the antiquities of Rome the Tuscan ornament on which I could base the formulation of the Canon," he had relied on Vitruvius.[1] As Branko Mitrovic explained in his edition of this treatise, "Vignola treats the orders as ornaments to be applied to the facade after the main dimensions of the building have been determined."[2]

Vitruvius had devoted one chapter in his *De architectura*—Book IV, chapter 2—specifically to the ornaments of the orders, while one of his primary aims in writing this treatise was to raise architecture to the level of rhetoric. This was the primary art of the ancient Greeks, his fundamental role model

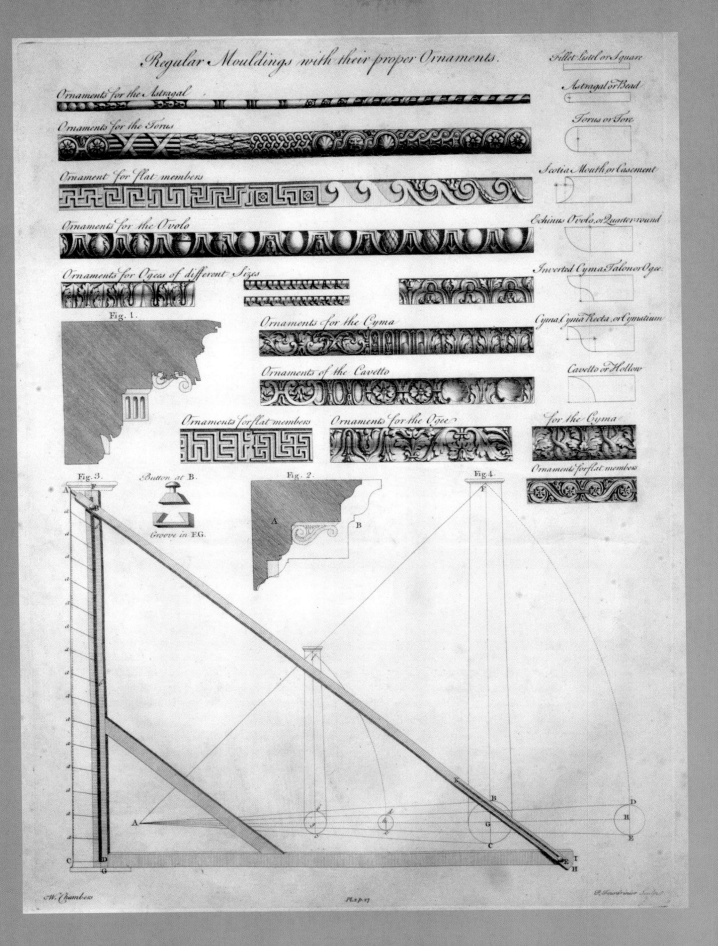

Regular Mouldings with their proper Ornaments.

Fillet Listel or Square

Ornaments for the Astragal

Astragal or Bead

Ornaments for the Torus

Torus or Tore

Ornament for flat members

Scotia Mouth or Casement

Ornaments for the Ovolo

Echinus Ovolo, or Quarter-round

Ornaments for Ogees of different Sizes

Inverted Cyma Talon or Ogee

Fig. 1.

Ornaments for the Cyma

Cyma, Cyma Recta, or Cymatium

Ornaments of the Cavetto

Cavetto or Hollow

Ornaments for flat members

Ornaments for the Ogee

for the Cyma

Fig. 3.

Button at B.

Fig. 2.

Fig. 4.

Groove in FG.

Ornaments for flat members

W. Chambers

Pl. 2 p. 27

P. Fourdrinier Sculp.t

which he interpreted through Cicero, citing his textbook on rhetoric, *De oratore*.[3] For Cicero, the "five parts of rhetoric" included *inventio*, which can be translated as eloquence, ornament, or style, Cicero going so far as to claim that the eloquence achieved by some architects was due to rhetoric rather than to the architectural profession.[4]

Leon Battista Alberti (1404–1472), who was inspired by Vitruvius yet aimed to improve on him, made ornament the subject of no less than four of the ten books of his great work, *De re aedificatoria*. The first of these was on ornament itself, and the next three on ornament to "Sacred Buildings," to "Public Secular Buildings," and to "Private Buildings." Alberti distinguished between beauty and ornament, beauty being "the intellectual and primary framework—the essential idea—while ornament is the phenomenon—the individual expression and embellishment of this frame."[5]

Beliefs of this kind prevailed until the birth of modernism in the twentieth century when, for example, Adolf Loos (1870–1933) published his influential rant, "Ornament and Crime" (1908). Believing that "Ornament is wasted labour and hence is wasted health," he claimed that because it is "no longer a natural product of our civilisation, it accordingly represents backwardness or degeneration." But he was confident that "we have conquered ornament, we have won through to lack of ornamentation," so that "no-one can create ornament now who lives on our level of culture." He came to the extraordinary conclusion that "lack of ornament is a sign of spiritual strength," even going so far as to argue, absurdly, that it was "lack of ornament" which accounted for the quality of Beethoven, whose "symphonies would never have been written by a man who was obliged to go about in silk, velvet and lace."

Such opposition to ornament has had a long life since 1908, but when sanity finally returned in some quarters in the late twentieth century it was given cogent expression in the writings on architecture of the philosopher Roger Scruton. He analyzed ornament and its importance with the following reference to the Corinthian order: "A naïve view of the Corinthian capital is that it is simply one of many possible ornaments to a column, and, like all ornaments, capable of elimination without excessive damage to the composition in which it features." He showed that this opinion is part of the misunderstanding that "the essence of the Order lies in geometrical ratios, and that its discipline can be recaptured by any similar system of proportion," of which he cited as an example the Modulor employed by Le Corbusier at his Unité de Habitation at Marseilles. Scruton claimed that by keeping "the mathematics of classical proportion, while rejecting significant detail, Corbusier retained what is accidental, while jettisoning all that is essential in the classical conception." Corbusier was, incidentally, a great admirer of Loos's "Ornament and Crime."

Scruton argued that the Corinthian capital, while undeniably ornamental, is no mere ornament, being "both the symbol of and the guide to the geometry which it crowns. The flowering of the stone in the capital requires the proportions of the column . . . The order is a system, not of geometry but of answerability: part answers part, length answers length, moulding answers moulding, throughout the vertical extent of the arrangement. The foliage receives the thrust of the column and cushions it against the abacus. The mouldings effectively divide the sections, and cast shadows which create a varying counterpoint to the fixed geometry. Everything is calculated to give maximum repose—the serene stillness of geometry—together with maximum variety—the play of light and shade, the impression of the carving hand, life revealed within the stone."[6]

Soon after Scruton's book came a revival of carved classical ornament and decoration in plaster, marble, and wood, though this was ironically aided by the loss of historic interiors in three disastrous fires between 1986 and 1992 at Hampton Court Palace, Uppark, and Windsor Castle (fig. 6.4; see figs. 4.5, 6).[7] It was initially considered virtually impossible to re-create these elaborate, fire-damaged interiors, partly because the promoters of modernism like Adolf Loos, who were opposed in principle to ornament, had long convinced the public that there were no longer any craftsmen with the requisite skills. Yet confronted with the challenge of re-creating these interiors accurately with the help of the thousands of fragments of ornament that had been gathered from the ashes, numerous artists and craftsmen, many of them young people anxious to learn new skills, came forward with enthusiasm to carry out this task, which they did with brilliant success and with considerable impact on subsequent projects.

For example, a happy offshoot was the publication in 2009 by the decorative plasterers Stevensons, Ltd., of Norwich, of *The National Trust Cornice Range*, an illustrated catalogue of extremely varied cornices described as from the "Early Georgian, Mid Georgian, Neo-Classical, and Regency periods." Dating from 1700 to 1840, all are taken from houses in the care of the National Trust and are available from Stevensons, who are employed by current classical architects such as Quinlan Terry and John Simpson.

THE ROLE OF MOLDINGS
AND THE ANALOGY WITH MUSIC

In the ornamental language of classical architecture and design, the orders are themselves enhanced with moldings which emphasize their profiles. The French architect and theorist Germain Boffrand (1667–1754) argued in 1745, "The profiles of buildings, and the other members that compose a building, are in architecture what words are in a discourse."[8] This was part of the novel interpretation of architecture in terms of character and style that Boffrand made with specific reference to Horace's Ars Poetica. Boffrand was soon followed by the Abbé Marc-Antoine Laugier

[6.4] *King's Privy Chamber, Hampton Court Palace, following restoration completed in 1990*

(1713–1769), who extended the parallel to music by arguing in his *Essai sur l'architecture* (1753) that:

"Round mouldings are to architecture what consonances are to musical harmony, whereas square mouldings correspond to dissonances. The blending of mouldings and of sounds has the same aim . . . [because] to create perfect harmony, the harshness of the square mouldings must from time to time interrupt the softness of the latter which could [otherwise] decline into insipid dullness . . . Then, the work will have nothing of dryness and the whole composition will be an enchanting sight."[9]

In this he was followed by Sir William Chambers (1723–1796), who published in 1759 *A Treatise on Civil Architecture*, which he later expanded as *A Treatise on the Decorative Part*

[6.5] *Dining room, Gonville and Caius College,*
Cambridge University, 1999, designed by John Simpson.
The ornamental treatment includes casts of the Bassae
frieze, as well as Corinthian and Ionic orders from Bassae.

of Civil Architecture (1791), one of the most attractive and thoughtful accounts of the orders ever written. Hailing Vitruvius as "the only remaining ancient writer upon the decorative part of architecture," Chambers claimed, "In the constructive part of architecture, the ancients do not seem to have been great proficients."[10] He thus treated the orders as a decorative, not constructive, part of architecture, explaining that he was "reserving for a future work those parts which relate to Convenience, Oeconomy and Strength." In thus separating the orders from function, Chambers followed Edmund Burke in his *Philosophical Enquiry into the Origin of our Ideas of the Sublime and Beautiful* (1757), where he opposed the functionalist belief that "the idea of utility, or of a part's being well adapted to answer its end, is the cause of beauty, or indeed beauty itself."[11]

After the opening section, "Of the Origin and Progress of Building," in Chambers's *Treatise*, he began the body of the book with extensive guidance on moldings, listed as ovolo, cyma recta, cyma reversa, cavetto, torus, astragal, scotia, and fillet, accompanying this with a useful plate, "Regular Mouldings with their Proper Ornaments" (fig. 6.3).[12] Having described all these moldings and their ornaments, Chambers concluded, "Hence it may be inferred, that there is something positive and natural, in these primary forms of architecture."[13] His disciple, Sir John Soane (1753–1837), believed that "mouldings are as essential and as important to the architect as colours to the painter," and elaborated on this point in his lectures at the Royal Academy, from 1809, where he claimed, "The art of profiling and enriching the different assemblages of mouldings, although now much neglected, is of the highest importance to the perfection of architecture. Perhaps the mind of a great artist is never more visible to the judicious observer than in this part of his profession, for profiles and assemblages of mouldings are in architecture similar and of equal importance with those indescribable elegancies in poetry and painting which are not always sufficiently felt nor duly appreciated."[14]

The moldings, which are appropriate to the various classical orders, have a curvaceous beauty of their own, imparting great variety and life to facades and interiors. Because this effect is enhanced by the changing shadows that they cast, their design involves knowledge of sciagraphy, derived from *skia*, the Greek word for shadow. It is the branch of the science of perspective dealing with the production of shadows that governs the whole process of ornamentation. Leonardo da Vinci stressed the fundamental importance of shadow when he claimed, "Shadow is the display (*pronuntiatione*) by bodies of their form; and the form of bodies would give no impression of their quality without it."

The moldings not only serve a decorative purpose but can themselves also be decorated. In the architecture of antiquity, about half of the moldings were normally enriched, though the Romans at their most lavish period during the Empire enriched all moldings. There are essentially five moldings, cyma recta, cyma reversa, ovolo, cavetto, and dentil, each of which can be ornamented with decoration such as egg and tongue, bead and reel, and waterleaf. This decoration might be compared to the enormous variety of the ornaments that feature so strongly in Renaissance and Baroque music. A further choice for the architect is to decide which parts of these enrichments should be gilded. Just as the basic elements of classical architecture are three, the column, entablature, and pediment, and are each divided into three units, so in music the sonata form, which appears in

[6.6] *Restoration of the interior of the Temple at Bassae, in C. R. Cockerell*, The Temples of Jupiter Panhellenius at Aegina, and of Apollo Epicurius at Bassae *(1860), "Interior of the Temple at Phigaleia"*

symphonies as well as sonatas, has three parts, an ABA rhythm of theme, development, and return. At the same time, the disciplines of architecture and music also have numerous flexible elements that bring variety to the basic core: for example, the Greek Doric column lacks a base just as a sonata does not invariably have only three movements.

The architect, educator, and theorist Jean-Nicolas-Louis Durand (1760–1834) echoed Laugier by pursuing the musical analogy when he observed in 1802 that architectural elements "exist within architecture like words in a discourse or notes in music."[15] Indeed, the grammar of the language of the orders is quite as complex as that of musical notation, so that in classical architecture the relation of every element to every other is based on a module, which is the diameter of the column at its foot. We can analyze this proportional relationship in the same way that we can analyze a Bach fugue in which the initial exposition or theme—a variant of the module in classical architecture—is heard successively in all the voices.

THE ROLE OF SCULPTURE

An important recent development has been the increasing understanding of the role of sculpture in classical architecture as can be seen in interiors by John Simpson, which show his understanding of ancient Greek architecture (fig. 6.5). His dining room at Gonville and Caius College, Cambridge (1999), not only incorporates casts of the figured frieze in the cella of the Temple of Apollo Epicurius at Bassae, but the whole configuration of the room is indebted to the paper restoration of that temple by the archaeologist and architect

Charles Robert Cockerell (1788–1863), who helped excavate it in 1811 (fig. 6.6). Cockerell was perhaps the first in modern times to be aware of the richness and freedom of Greek architecture, and especially of its sculptural basis. His staircase hall at Oakly Park, Shropshire (1823–24), incorporated souvenirs of his discoveries in Greece, including a top-lit cast of the Bassae frieze (fig. 6.7). In his additions of 1845–47 at the Fitzwilliam Museum, Cambridge, he adorned the drum supporting his cupola in the staircase hall with straining telamons derived from the unusual figure sculpture of the Temple of Jupiter Olympius at Agrigentum, Sicily, in the excavation of which he had played a part (fig. 6.8).[16]

Cockerell believed with Michelangelo in the Greek view of sculpture as "the voice of architecture, the soul of her expression" and was aware that Greek architectural ornament and figure sculpture encapsulated a vital human presence, including entasis, tapering, inclination, thickening. He pointed to Michelangelo's fragment of an undated letter referring to the symmetry of the human body, nose in the center of the face balanced by matching eyes, and hands which must match each other, to which Michelangelo added, "And surely the architectural members derive from human members. Whoever has not been or is not a good master of the figure and likewise of anatomy cannot understand anything of architecture." Current sculptors who contribute to this tradition include Dick Reid and especially Alexander Stoddart, whose narrative friezes inspired by Homer's *Odyssey* and *Iliad* feature prominently in the entrance hall of the new Queen's Gallery at Buckingham Palace by John Simpson of 2002 (fig. 6.9). The Scottish Parliament appointed Stoddart as Sculptor in Ordinary to Her Majesty The Queen in Scotland in 2009.

[6.8] *C. R. Cockerell, Fitzwilliam Museum, Cambridge, 1845–47, interior of cupola in entrance hall.* Photograph courtesy *Country Life*

[6.9 OPPOSITE] *Queen's Gallery, Buckingham Palace, 2002, designed by John Simpson. The entrance hall includes friezes and winged genii by sculptor Alexander Stoddart.* Royal Collection Trust / © Her Majesty Queen Elizabeth II 2013

PAINTED INTERIORS

The paintings of ancient Rome, mostly known from domestic interiors in Pompeii, Herculaneum, and other towns in the Bay of Naples, included illusionistic architectural and garden scenes. They were not rediscovered until the eighteenth century, though Andrea Mantegna (c. 1431–1506) painted a remarkably inventive *capriccio* of Rome in the scene *The Meeting* in his Camera degli Sposi in the Palazzo Ducale at Mantua (fig. 6.10; figs. 1.29, 30). Depicting the return of Cardinal Francesco Gonzaga to Mantua from Rome, this included the Aurelian Walls, Colosseum, Arch of Titus, Pyramid of Caius Cestius, Theatre of Marcellus, Aqua Claudia (the most ambitious of Rome's aqueducts), the still well preserved Ponte Nomentano, and ruins of the Domus Flavia on the Quirinal. Even more strikingly on a hill outside the walls, Mantegna depicted a white, pedimented building with a ground-floor colonnade, a classical design in which he came close to anticipating Palladio's Palazzo Chiericati.

In the revival of painted interiors as part of the Neoclassical movement in eighteenth-century England, the Florentine artist Giovanni Battista Cipriani (1727–1785) played a key role. While in Rome, he met William Chambers, who brought him to England, where he became a Foundation Member of the Royal Academy in 1768 and was much employed by Chambers as a decorative painter. Cipriani's parlor at Standlynch (now Trafalgar) House, Wiltshire, of c. 1766, has a continuous landscape on all four walls, inhabited by gods and temples (fig. 6.11).[17]

[6.12 OPPOSITE] *The Neoclassical wall paintings in Setton House by Renzo Mongiardino depict classical ruins, armorial elements, and classical figures.*

[6.13 FOLLOWING PAGES] *A seascape mural by artist Anne Harris adorns the dining room designed by Priscilla Ullmann, interior designer.*

The dazzling Pompeian Gallery of 1785–88 at Packington Hall, Warwickshire, by the Italian architect Joseph Bonomi, was executed by a team of mainly Italian craftsmen and decorators.[18] More native products, associated with the rise of the Picturesque in England, were painted interiors such as that by Paul Sandby of 1793 at Drakelowe Hall, Derbyshire, including a clearing in a forest opening onto a river valley with a tower, perhaps inspired by a painting by Claude Lorrain.[19] The staircase at Bretton Park, Yorkshire, was dramatically painted in c. 1815 with trompe l'oeil classical buildings and ruins, attributed to Agostino Aglio, which can be seen as a remote descendant of Mantegna's *capriccio* at Mantua.

The Italian architect Renzo Mongiardino (1916–1998) was one of the most inventive and romantic of all designers of illusionistic interiors, including in his case faux marble and intarsia, and simulated wall hangings (fig. 6.12).[20] Drawing on sources ranging from ancient Rome to the Empire style, he employed a team of painters, gilders, carpenters, and model makers, who moved effortlessly from working on his sets for stage and screen to interiors in real buildings. His creations have an unparalleled magic.

The American muralist Anne Harris, who established a studio in 1985, has a varied oeuvre that includes a dining room in a residence in New York with walls painted with a watery Long Island seascape that echoes the tradition of Cipriani's parlor at Standlynch (fig. 6.13). Quinlan Terry's son and partner, Francis, is also a talented artist who painted a large panoramic backdrop in 2010 for the theater they built at Downing College, Cambridge, in 2009–10. In the tradition of the *capriccio*, it includes the Acropolis and its monuments as well as designs by William Wilkins, original architect of the college in 1806.

There is perhaps still no better guide to the significance of ornament in civilization than *The Grammar of Ornament* by Owen Jones (1856). This sumptuously illustrated publication by the architect and ornamental designer who created the Egyptian, Greek, Roman, and Alhambra Courts at the Crystal Palace contains essays that are both scholarly and practical by various hands, including Joseph Bonomi Jr., James Wild, Christopher Dresser, and Matthew Digby Wyatt. It begins with the guiding principle that "the Decorative Arts arose from, and should properly be attendant upon Architecture," and goes on to explain, "Whenever any style of ornament commands universal admiration, it will always be found to be in accordance with the laws which regulate the distribution of form in nature . . . Man appears everywhere impressed with the beauties of nature which surround him and seeks to imitate to the extent of his power the works of the Creator."

The practitioners and theorists of modernism believed they had abolished the past where, as Jones put it, "from the universal testimony of travellers, it would appear that there is scarcely a people in however early a stage of civilisation with whom the desire for ornament is not a strong instinct."[21] Though modernist doctrines are responsible for the inhumanity of most present-day buildings which lack moldings or ornament, the illustrations in the present book indicate the reassuring extent to which the tide has turned.

CHAPTER SEVEN

PROPORTIONS OF INTERIORS

RICHARD SAMMONS

[7.1] *The double cube room at Wilton near Salisbury, England, was designed c. 1653 by Inigo Jones and John Webb. The dimensions of the room are 30 feet by 60 feet with a ceiling height of 30 feet.*

Few will disagree of the importance of good proportions, but achieving it in design is often illusive, even for seasoned designers. As an aesthetic phenomenon, it is something that all can recognize, but why it works has led to numerous and seemingly contradictory conclusions, and spurious theories abound. The one thing that is clear is that we are speaking of a physical phenomenon. We respond to an object as beautiful because of its physical characteristics, of which one fundamental component are the proportional relationships.

Proportion in architecture is the art of adjusting the size and shape of elements within a design such that they look good in relationship to each other and to the work as a whole. In the design of the best classical works there are a limited series of related numerical ratios that repeat from larger to smaller scale, determining the size of each element. The ratios between the height, width, and length of every volume are repeated in the shape of window and doors, wall paneling, even the individual panes of glass. The size and shape of every architectural element, columns, entablatures, dados, the size and projection of every molding is related to everything else. Each element holds the proportional information of the whole and vice versa, like the DNA in our individual cells. The architect who takes on this task is playing what Sir Edwin

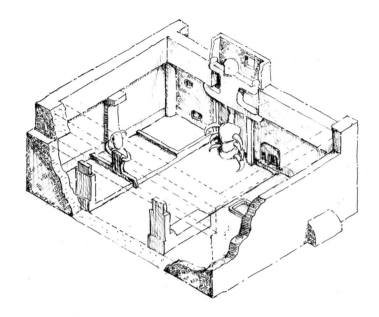

[7.3] *Çatal Hüyük, neolithic shrine of unexpected sophistication, 7500 BCE to 5700 BCE, drawing by Richard Sammons*

Lutyens called "the great game, the high game of architecture." Granted, few have risen to this "great game" and, as in any such human endeavor, realities conspire against us. But even to remotely approach this goal, the enormity of the task would be insurmountable, unless some system of proportion is employed.

The setting out of proportions of interiors is multifaceted and generally much more difficult than designing a plan or facade. A room has normally at least four facades, not counting the often neglected planes of the ceiling and floor. The shape of the volume of the room must be considered and should relate to the divisions of the walls, ceiling, and floor. Generally one starts with the shape and form of the volume.

The proportioning of the volume of a room has been treated in a number of different ways. It is easy to conceive of volumes as the inverse of recognizable solids such as a cube (fig. 7.2), a double cube (fig. 7.1), a cylinder, or in combination such as the half sphere over a cylinder of the same

height that defines the volume of the interior of the Pantheon (see fig. 1.16), but these simple forms, though perfect for special rooms and monumental interiors, do not provide the variety of shape necessary or practical for the design of complex interiors. Volumetrically the proportion of the rooms along with the delicacies of relating walls to plan has typological meanings. Corridors are long and skinny implying movement, whereas square rooms are places of pause or focus. Vestibules are typically square to imply a stop in movement through the sequence of rooms. Square or regular polygons of larger size work well for indicating center, such as the rotunda of the United States Capitol, or on a domestic scale providing focus for an inward-looking room, such as an intimate dining room or study. Loggia and porches should not be so deep as to be rooms unto themselves but shallow so that the occupants can engage with the out-of-doors projected into the landscape. Most other functions are generally rectangular, from a double square for a two-seating group living room to squarer plans for more condensed furniture groupings. The proportional setting out of volumes is outside the scope of this chapter; it will suffice to say it takes great care as each room is experienced in relation to other rooms, and the volumes of these rooms must nest together within the overall form of the building.

Therefore, for the sake of simplicity we will start with the design of one elevation of a typical "Georgian Room." In Georgian times it was the practice to simply superimpose an order on the wall and carry the details around the room making deletions to be in keeping with the level of dignity appropriate to the room's use. Though this approach will yield a perfectly acceptable classical interior it will do little to shed light on the principles of proportion employed when the architectural order was first designed.

To do this we need only to understand the bare bones of proportional theory, a subject that can get very arcane very quickly. Simply put, proportion comes down to portioning out, dividing up. If we take a simple segment of a line, as an example, this is easy to demonstrate. These proportions need to be thought of in qualitative compositional terms, equal versus unequal, center versus edge.

First, one could simply divide the segment in half, making two equal subsegments. As they are equal, neither one is hierarchically greater than the other. This condition is called duality. This condition is generally unsatisfying, as the parts being equal are in conflict; neither one dominates the other.

|————|————|

If this process continues and the subsegments are divided in half and so on, we create certain monotony, in two dimensions nothing but a grid. Modern architecture has in the past emphasized the grid as a "rational approach," but surely there is a little art in this. Now say we push this center line division over to one side a bit. This inflection will produce two recognizably different sized subsegments. This implied movement gives life to the stagnant grid. Unequal division is used by architects and artists to move the eye around the composition. The ratio of this unequal division is called differentiation. A ratio is chosen and is fixed, setting up an expectation which is helpfully rewarded from large- to small-scale details. Among the more famous ratios chosen for this compositional task is the Golden Section, an irrational ratio of 1:1.614 . . . , though in our Georgian room we can round this off to 3:5 or 5:8 or any number pair in the equally famous Fibonnaci series,[1] which approximates the irrational ratio of Golden Section in a whole-number (though inexact) geometric progression. To Renaissance architects this ratio for differentiation was unresolved and somewhat in dispute, and the simple arithmetic mean, geometric mean, and harmonic mean were used, sometimes all together as in Palladio's recommended heights of rooms. But the actual ratio is somewhat unimportant; anything between ⅝ and ¾ will do as long as it is obvious to the eye that they are clearly unequal but not so unequal as to suggest an edge. The important part is that this ratio repeats as often as practical from larger to smaller scale.

|——————|————|

Finally, after creating this movement, it is necessary to stop the eye, to punctuate the composition. Returning to our segment of a line we now move over the point of division far over to the edge such that in two dimensions this much smaller subsegment would form a picture frame around the rectangle.

|——————————|——|

This is the ratio of punctuation that will dictate the size of those edge elements of the composition.[2]

If we return to our example of the Georgian room we see that the wall is bracketed vertically by the dado or socle and the entablature that forms the horizontal members of the architectural order, and often vertical divisions indicated by paneling or in the highest examples pilasters or engaged columns. This is derived from Roman and Greek work, but the pattern is far older. One of the earliest interiors we know of is that of the shrine at Çatal Hüyük (fig. 7.3). Here the pattern of a band defining the top of the wall as well as a socle defining the base are already established. Vertically, the wall is divided by pilasters, and the floor is patterned by lines drawn into a nine-square grid. The wall elements are clearly in imitation of structural elements but are purely decorative, a fiction so to speak. This fictive structure remained a key part of the decoration of walls for millennia and persists to this day.

In our Georgian room the cornice and other architectural details are executed as wood or plaster "trim." In addition to disguising constructional joints, trim helps to punctuate each element of the room: the crown and baseboard signal that the wall is ending and the floor or ceiling is beginning; casings signal that the wall surface is about to be interrupted by a door or window opening. Figure 7.4 demonstrates the use of trim to punctuate the room, yet the sizes of trim are all iden-

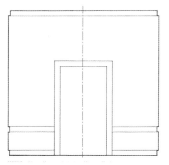

[7.4] *Trim providing punctuation but not differentiated by size*

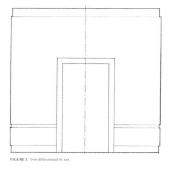

[7.5] *Trim differentiated by size*

[7.6] *Trim differentiated by size and character*

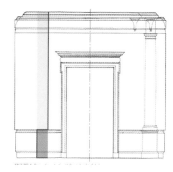

[7.7] *Ratio of punctuation (1:5) sets height of dado*

tical and are therefore unable to indicate their different uses. However, *differentiation* can be introduced by modulating either the size of the moldings (fig. 7.5) or their character (fig. 7.6).

Figure 7.7 shows a typical Georgian interior, an analysis of which is useful because it embodies all the elements of a classical order in a succinct and interrelated fashion. Note the column, pedestal, and entablature superimposed to the right of the door. The actual presence of this column is not absolutely necessary within the interior, yet it helps demon-

strate the way in which the orders can extend to all areas and scales of design.

To begin, we first establish a dado or datum, from which the proportions of the room's details are generated according to the particular order being employed. The ratio of punctuation usually sets the height of the dado, which determines the relation of the chair rail to the total height of the room (fig. 7.7). While it is ideal to set the height of the dado in this manner, often a low ceiling height necessitated by the exigencies of construction makes this impossible. In this case,

[7.8] *Entablature is punctuated*

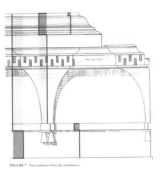

[7.10] *Punctuations within the entablature*

[7.9] *Punctuations of baseboard, casing, door entablature, and ceiling trim*

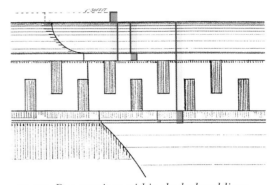

[7.11] *Punctuations within the bed moldings*

the dado should be set at two feet, ten inches or a similarly practical height.

Following the placement of the dado, a punctuating move upward sets the height of the entablature. This determines the relationship between the size of the entablature and the room height (fig. 7.8). Even though the sizes determined by these two punctuations are different, both repeat the same ratio. Punctuation also sets the size of the skirt (baseboard), the chair rail, the height of the door's entablature above the chair rail, and the size of the architrave as it moves down the

sides of the doorway. It also informs the placement of any bounding trim on the ceiling (fig. 7.9). The same ratio of punctuation is also applied to the details of the entablature: the architrave to the complete entablature, the taenia to the architrave, etc. (fig. 7.10). Likewise, punctuation is used to determine the sizes and relationships between even the smallest details of the interior (fig. 7.11).

Differentiation also plays an important role in the design of the interior. The first differentiating move should be to determine the size and location of the most important dis-

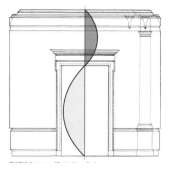

[7.12] *Door opening differentiated from wall surface*

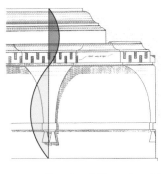

[7.14] *Cornice differentiated from architrave and frieze*

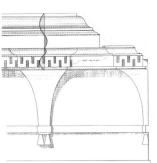

[7.16] Cymation *differentiated from* corona; ovolo *differentiated from Wall of Troy*

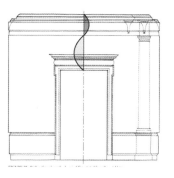

[7.13] *Wall surface above the door differentiated from the entablature*

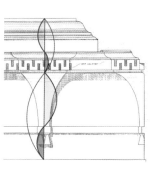

[7.15] Cymation *and* corona *differentiated from bed mold; frieze differentiated from architrave*

tinction in the composition at hand: in this case, the violent act of opening a doorway in the wall is the most significant. Therefore, a ratio of differentiation will determine the height of the doorway in relation to the height of the room (fig. 7.12). Similarly, the same ratio is used to set the bottom of the entablature above the doorway (fig. 7.13). Within the entablature, the proud cornice is more elaborate than the simple architrave and frieze; therefore, it too is differentiated (fig. 7.14). Figure 7.15 differentiates the *cymatium* and *corona* from the bed molds below them; the frieze is also differentiated from the architrave. Likewise, the *cymatium* is differ-

entiated from the corona, and the ovolo from the wall of Troy dentil course (fig. 7.16). Even the solid and void portions of the wall of Troy are differentiated, as is the solid to the fillet below (fig. 7.17). Differentiation is also applied horizontally (fig. 7.18).

Although no dualities (equal-equal relationships) were purposefully designed, the repetition of like ratios will inevitably result in some equal elements. However, in this case the greatly differing characters of the cornice and frieze provide a measure of differentiation that alleviates their equal size (fig. 7.19).

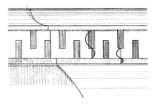

[7.17] *Differentiated within the Wall of Troy*

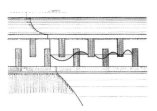

[7.18] *Horizontal differentiations within the Wall of Troy*

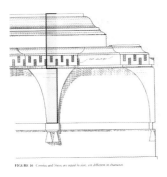

[7.19] *Cornice and frieze equal in size yet different in character*

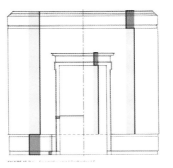

[7.20] *Ratio of punctuation set at 1:7 rather than 1:5*

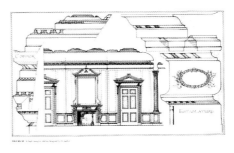

[7.21] *A high Georgian interior designed by the author*

We can, of course, alter our set ratios. The preceding illustrations used a ratio of punctuation set at 1:5, yet figure 7.20 shows a similar interior designed using a punctuating ratio of 1:7. It should be obvious that scaling the ratios of both punctuation and differentiation has a great effect on the character of an interior, resulting in a room we might call Neoclassical in flavor (fig. 7.21). The proportion set for differentiation may also be varied, imparting a gradient of characters.

Today proportion remains a muddled and misunderstood subject among architects. Discredited Renaissance theories seeking to link proportion to the cosmic order, musical harmony, or the human body are still repeated, ignoring centuries of continued inquiry. Despite its importance, the subject has been mostly neglected in recent decades by major schools of architecture. But without it, the student is left to intuition, and their work is merely willfullness and fancy uninformed by objective visual reason as bases on a priori truths. Proportional theory will not design for you but is a harmonizing tool to bring the diverse elements of a composition into tune. Untethered to composition, it simply produces meaningless patterns; without evidence of intelligent intention, like Mandelbrot's fractals, it will yield little more than a pleasant monotony.

NOTES

CHAPTER ONE
SURVEY OF CLASSICAL INTERIOR DESIGN

1 Mitchell Owens, "Renzo Mongiardino Dies at 81; Designer with Flair for Illusion," *New York Times*, February 2, 1998.

2 Fiorenza Cattaneo, ed., *Roomscapes: The Decorative Architecture of Renzo Mongiardino* (New York: Rizzoli, 1993), 15.

3 The history of current classicism is covered with a somewhat different approach in the introduction to my earlier work on this subject, *New Classicism: The Rebirth of Traditional Architecture* (New York: Rizzoli, 2004).

4 For further exploration of the prodigious history of classical design, a comprehensive list of books may be found in the resources of the Institute of Classical Architecture & Art at www.classicist.org.

5 Detailed explanation of the elements of the orders is the subject of numerous books including: Robert Chitham, *The Classical Orders of Architecture* (New York: Rizzoli, 1985) and William R. Ware, *The American Vignola: A Guide to the Making of Classical Architecture* (New York: Dover, 1994).

6 Vitruvius, *The Ten Books of Architecture*, trans. Morris Hickey Morgan (New York: Dover Publications, 1960), 103 (Book IV, Chapter 6).

7 Ibid., 103–4 (Book IV, Chapter 7).

8 Thomas Gordon Smith, *Vitruvius on Architecture* (New York: Monacelli, 2003), 99.

9 Details of entasis may be found in numerous modern texts including two translations of Vitruvius with detailed notations by Thomas Gordon Smith and a second by Ingrid D. Rowland and Thomas Noble Howe.

10 Additional information on visual refinements employed in the construction of Greek temples is covered in J. J. Coulton, *Ancient Greek Architects at Work: Problems of Structure and Design* (Ithaca, N.Y.: Cornell University Press, 1991).

11 The cella was the internal room used to house the cult statue and altar.

12 John W. Stamper, *The Architecture of Roman Temples* (Cambridge, Mass.: Cambridge University Press, 2005), 198. The most thorough coverage of the Pantheon is available in Kjeld De Fine Licht, *The Rotunda in Rome: A Study of Hadrian's Pantheon* (Copenhagen: Jutland Archaeological Society, 1968).

13 Fikert Yegul, *Baths and Bathing in Classical Antiquity* (Cambridge, Mass.: MIT Press, 1992), 30. Much information concerning Roman baths is found in this source.

14 Yegul, 164. Size of the complex given as 120,000 square meters.

15 J. B. Ward-Perkins, *Roman Imperial Architecture* (London: Penguin, 1981), 419.

16 Shirley Johnston, *Great Villas of the Riviera* (New York: Rizzoli, 1998), 88–97.

17 Leon Battista Alberti, *On the Art of Building in Ten Books*, trans. Joseph Rykwert et al. (Cambridge, Mass.: MIT Press, 1988), 154 (Book 6, Chapter 1).

18 Alberti, 156 (Book 6, Chapter 2).

19 Alberti, 152–53 (Book 5, Chapter 18). Boreas is the north wind.

20 Robert Tavernor and Richard Schofield, *Andrea Palladio: The Four Books of Architecture* (Cambridge, Mass.: MIT Press, 1998), xvii.

CHAPTER TWO
GRAND TOUR AS INFLUENCE ON NEOCLASSICAL DESIGN

1 Alan and Ann Gore, *The History of English Interiors* (London: Phaidon, 1995), 68.

2 Christopher Hibbert, *The Grand Tour* (London: Methuen, 1987), 242.

3 Andrew Wilton and Ilaria Bignamini, *Grand Tour: The Lure of Italy in the Eighteenth Century* (London: Tate Gallery, 1996), 27.

4 The Museo Pio Clementino, Vatican, Rome (1771–94) was begun in 1771 under Clement XIV (Giovanni Vincenzo Ganganelli, Pope 1769–74) and finished under Pius VI (Gianangelo Braschi, Pope 1775–99). Wilton and Bignamini, 241.

5 Frank Salmon, *Building on Ruins* (Aldershot: Ashgate, 2000), 53.

6 Wilton and Bignamini, 27, 39, and 137.

7 Hibbert, 238.

8. Peter Thornton, *Form & Decoration: Innovation in the Decorative Arts 1470–1870* (London: Weidenfeld & Nicolson, 1998), 155; Wilton and Bignamini, 40. The German scholar and most respected authority on Roman antiques in the eighteenth century, Johann Joachim Winckelmann (1717–1768), served as Albani's librarian and artistic adviser. Wilton and Bignamini, 174 and 212.

9 Hibbert, 180. Portraits were considerably cheaper in Rome than in England. Wilton and Bignamini, 52.

10 Wilton and Bignamini, 85.

11 Hibbert, 242.

12 Olive Cook, *The English House through Seven Centuries* (New York: Overlook, 1968), 193; Campbell designed Wanstead, Essex, the first great Palladian Revival house in England. Gore, 61.

13 Hibbert, 193; Robin Fedden and Rosemary Joekes, *The National Trust Guide* (London: National Trust, 1973), 36.

14 The English poet Alexander Pope praised the work of Burlington and Kent at Chiswick, saying: "Erect new wonders and the old repair:/Jones and Palladio to themselves restore/And be whatever Vitruvius was before." Excerpt from the fourth of the *Moral Essays* Pope dedicated to Lord Burlington. Cook, 202.

15 Summerson, 342.

16 Stuart and Revett issued *Proposals for Publishing an Accurate Description of the Antiquities in Athens* in 1748 and by 1751 had secured funding from the Society of Dilettanti to finance their study-tour. Subsequently, the Society sponsored the publication of their drawings as *The Antiquities of Athens*, in 1762. Thornton, *Form and Decoration*, 177.

17 Thornton, 177.

18 John Martin Robinson, *Spencer House* (London: Spencer House, 2006), 2. Spencer became a member of the Society of the Dilettanti in 1765.

19 Alan and Ann Gore, 68.

20 David Watkin, *Athenian Stuart: Pioneer of the Greek Revival* (London: George Alan and Unwin, 1982), 35.

21 Watkin, 36.

22 Watkin, 39; Robinson, 30.

23 Robinson, 30. The Loggie is the second of three connected arcades envisioned by Julius II and begun by Donato Bramante in 1508. Only the first arcade was finished when Bramante died in 1514, and the commission was given to Raphael, who completed the arcades, beginning the decoration in of the loggia that bears his name in 1517 and finishing the scheme that features grotesques and arabesques patterned on ancient Roman motifs in 1519. *Guide to the Vatican Museums and City* (Vatican City: Gestione Vendita Pubblicazioni Musei Vaticani, 1986), 79.

24 Watkin, 38.

25 Watkin, 39.

26 Examples include Holkham Hall, Dunham Massey, Farnborough Hall, Felbrigg Hall, Houghton Hall, Uppark, and Spencer House, all built or reconstructed in the eighteenth century and furnished with art acquired on the Grand Tour. Hibbert, 242; also, see the individual listings in *The National Trust Guide*.

27 Robert Wood, *Ruins of Palmyra* (1753), *Ruins of Balbec* (1757); Stuart and Revett, *The Antiquities of Athens* (1762); Comte de Caylus, *Recueil d'antiquités* (1752); Winckelmann, *Gedanken über die Nachahmung der griechischen Werke* (1755); J. D. Le Roy, *Les Ruines des plus beaux monuments de la Grèce* (1758); Piranesi, *Prima parte di architettura e prospettive* (1743), *Vedute di Roma* (1745), *Antichità romane* (1748), Carceri (1750), *Trofei di Ottaviano Augusto* (1753), *Della magnificenza ed architettura de' Romani* (1761), *Parere su l'architettura* (1765), and *Diverse maniere d' adornare I cammini* (1769).
28 Geoffrey Beard, *The Work of Robert Adam* (London: Bloomsbury Books, 1978), 229.
29 Salmon, 20.
30 Hibbert, 248.

CHAPTER THREE
CLASSICAL REVIVAL
IN THE NINETEENTH AND TWENTIETH CENTURIES

1 Talbot Hamlin, *Greek Revival Architecture in America* (London: Oxford University Press, 1944), 318.
2 Donald Drew Egbert, *The Beaux-Arts Tradition in French Architecture* (Princeton: Princeton University Press, 1980), 99.
3 Details of instruction changed through the almost three hundred years of the Ecole's existence, and detailed information may be found in Egbert's book as well as Arthur Drexler, ed., *The Architecture of the Ecole des Beaux-Arts* (New York: Museum of Modern Art), 1977.
4 In addition to MIT, by 1900 programs of architecture were established at Cornell University, University of Illinois, Syracuse University, University of Michigan, Columbia University, University of Pennsylvania, Columbian College (now George Washington University), Armour Institute (now Illinois Institute of Technology), and Harvard University.
5 Charles Follen McKim (1847–1909), Edward Pearce Casey (1864–1940), John Merven Carrère (1858–1911), Thomas Hastings (1860–1929), Arthur Brown, Jr. (1874–1957), John Russell Pope (1874–1937), Julia Morgan (1872–1957), and Whitney Warren (1864–1941).

CHAPTER FOUR
RE-CREATING THE PAST

1 John Ruskin, *The Seven Lamps of Architecture* (New York: Dover, 1989), 178. This Dover edition is a republication of the second edition of the work published in 1880. The first edition was published in 1849.
2 Christopher Rowell and John Martin Robinson, *Uppark Restored* (London: National Trust, 1996), 44.
3 Ibid., 166.
4 Elizabeth D. Mulloy, *The History of the National Trust for Historic Preservation*, Washington, D.C.: Preservaiton Press, 1976), 12.
5 Brent Brolin, *Architecture in Context* (New York: Van Nostrand Reinhold, 1980), 7. Quoted in Norman Tyler, Historic Preservation (New York: Norton, 2000), 139.

JOHN MILNER ARCHITECTS

1 Written document provided by the office titled "Veranda Presents… The Art of the Design Awards Candidate Form": John Milner Architects, Inc.
2 Annabel Hsin, "Nemours' Comeback," *Traditional Building*, June 2011, 25.

BRUNO AND ALEXANDRE LAFOURCADE

1 "A Place in Provence." *Robb Report*, September 1, 2005. http://robbreport.com/A-Place-In-Provence.aspx

DONALD INSALL ASSOCIATES

1 Donald Insall. *Living Buildings: Architectural Conservation; Philosophy, Principles, and Practice*. Australia: Images Publishing (2008), 10.

CHAPTER FIVE
THE REVIVAL OF MODERN CLASSICISM
THROUGH EDUCATION OF DESIGNERS AND CRAFTSMEN

1 Paul Goldberger, "Allan Greenberg's Rooms in the Department of State," *Antiques*, July 1987, 133.
2 *Allan Greenberg: Selected Works* (London: Academy Editions, 1995), 37.
3 Philippe de Montebello, foreword to *The New Nineteenth-Century European Paintings and Sculpture Galleries*, by Gary Tinterow (New York: Metropolitan Museum of Art, 1993), 5.
4 Gary Tinterow, *The New Nineteenth-Century European Paintings and Sculpture Galleries* (New York: Metropolitan Museum of Art, 1993), 27.
5 Henrika Taylor, et al., eds., *A Decade of Art & Architecture 1992–2002* (New York: ICA/CA, 2003), 6.
6 Architects in America who taught a variety of classical design courses include John Blatteau at the University of Pennsylvania and Drexel University, Elizabeth Dowling at the Georgia Institute of Technology, Francois Gabriel at Syracuse University, Allan Greenberg at Yale and Columbia Universities, and Robert A. M. Stern at Columbia and Yale Universities.
7 Jane A. Devine, ed., *100 Years of Architecture at Notre Dame* (South Bend, Ind.: University of Notre Dame, 1999), 61.
8 T-Square clubs were popular in the first decades of the twentieth century. They were loosely organized evening schools for draftsmen without college educations. Skills in design were taught by practicing architects who enjoyed the social aspect of reliving their college days in the studio or their own time at the Ecole des Beaux-Arts.
9 Henrika Taylor, et al., *A Decade of Art & Architecture*, 9.
10 The course list includes both permanent annual courses and elective offerings. Among the courses offered are the study of the orders, ornamental plaster, geometric proportioning, theories of classical architecture, and drawing courses in watercolor, oil, and pencil.
11 Written interview, Clem Labine, on November 15, 2011.

ALLAN GREENBERG, ARCHITECT

1 Allan Greenberg, "The Architecture of Democracy," *New Classicism* (New York: Rizzoli International, 1990), 69–72, and Allan Greenberg, *George Washington Architect* (London: Andreas Papadakis Publisher, 1999)
2 Arthur Lubow, "The Ionic Man," *Departures*, May-June 1999, 156–57.
3 Allan Greenberg, "The Architecture of Democracy," *New Classicism* (New York: Rizzoli International, 1990), 72.

STUDIO PEREGALLI

1 First edition written in Italian with subsequent translations in French and English.
2 Laura Sartori Rimini and Roberto Peregalli, *The Invention of the Past: Interior Design and Architecture of Studio Peregalli* (New York: Rizzoli, 2011), 15.

NOTES

ERNESTO BUCH ARCHITECT
1 Written interview with Ernesto Buch, June 15, 2012.
2 Written interview with Ernesto Buch, April 6, 2012.

DE LA GUARDIA VICTORIA ARCHITECTS & URBANISTS
1 From DLGV Practice Philosophy and Biographies, 2012.
2 Ibid., 1.

APPLETON & ASSOCIATES
1 *New Classicist: Appleton & Associates Architects* (Images Publishing, 2007), 16.
2 Written interview, Marc Appleton, April 22, 2012.
3 *New Classicist: Appleton & Associates Architects*, 17.

HISTORICAL CONCEPTS
1 James Lowell Strickland and Susan Sully, *Coming Home: The Southern Vernacular House* (New York: Rizzoli, 2012), 27.
2 Ibid., 34.

J. P. MOLYNEUX STUDIO
1 Michael Frank, *Molyneux: The Interior Design of Juan Pablo Molyneux* (New York: Rizzoli), 11.
2 Ibid., 9.

CRAIG HAMILTON ARCHITECTS
1 Gavin Stamp, foreword to *Craig Hamilton: Architectural Drawings, Furniture, and Models* (London: The Gallery Cork Street, 2009), 5.
2 Written interview, Craig Hamilton, June 6, 2012.

QUINLAN & FRANCIS TERRY ARCHITECTS
1 Taken from a speech given at the Oxford Union Debate, November 1987. Published in *The Salisbury Review*, June 1988. *Quinlan Terry: Selected Works* (London: Academy Editions, 1993), 132.

JULIAN BICKNELL & ASSOCIATES
1 Written interview, Julian Bicknell, April 2, 2012.
2 Julian Bicknell. introduction to *Julian Bicknell: Designs and Buildings 1980–2000* (Richmond-Upon-Thames, UK: Julian Bicknell & Associates, 2000).

JOHN SIMPSON & PARTNERS
1 Richard John and David Watkin, *John Simpson: The Queen's Gallery, Buckingham Palace and Other Works* (London: Andreas Papadakis, 2002), 11.
2 Ibid., 14.

FAIRFAX & SAMMONS ARCHITECTS
1 Eve M. Kahn, "Lyrical Compositions," *Period Homes* 4, no. 1 (Spring 2003): 10.

DAVID JONES ARCHITECTS
1 Written interview, David Jones, May 31, 2012.

G. P. SCHAFER ARCHITECT
1 Written interview, Gil Schafer, June 19, 2012.
2 Ibid.
3 Ibid.

FERGUSON & SHAMAMIAN ARCHITECTS
1 Written interview, Mark Ferguson, June 28, 2012.

ROBERT A. M. STERN ARCHITECTS
1 *Robert A.M. Stern Buildings* (New York: Monacelli Press, 1996), 17.

CHAPTER SIX
ORNAMENT: A SOURCE OF BEAUTY
1 Giacomo Barozzi da Vignola, *Canon of the Five Orders of Architecture*, with introduction by David Watkin (New York: Dover, 2011), caption to pl. 4.
2 Vignola, op. cit., trans. Branko Mitrovic (New York: Acanthus Press, 1999), 17.
3 Vitruvius, *De Architectura*, trans. F. Granger (Cambridge, Mass.: Harvard University Press, 1885), 17, (Vol. II, Book IX, preface).
4 Cicero, *De oratore*, vol. I, 62.
5 Leon Battista Alberti, *On the Art of Building in Ten Books*, trans. J. Rykwert, N. Leach, and R. Tavernor (Cambridge, Mass.: MIT Press, 1988), 420.
6 Roger Scruton, *The Aesthetic Understanding* (Manchester, UK: Carcanet Press, 1983), 215–16.
7 See Simon Thurley, *Hampton Court: A Social and Architectural History* (New Haven and London: Yale University Press, 2003), 383–86; Christopher Rowell and John Martin Robinson, *Uppark Restored* (London: National Trust, 1996); and Adam Nicolson, *Restoration: The Rebuilding of Windsor Castle* (London: Michael Joseph with The Royal Collection, 1997).
8 Germain Boffrand, *Livre d'Architecture contenant les principes généraux de cet art* (Paris: G. Cavelier, 1745), 22.
9 Marc-Antoine Laugier, *An Essay on Architecture*, trans. Wolfgang and Anni Herrmann (Los Angeles: Hennessey & Ingalls, 1977), 43.
10 William Chambers, *A Treatise on the Decorative Part of Civil Architecture* (London: Joseph Smeeton, 1791), 17, 23.
11 Edmund Burke, *Philosophical Enquiry into the Origin of our Ideas of the Sublime and Beautiful*, 5th ed. (London: J. Dodsley, 1767), 191.
12 Quinlan Terry's discovery of this plate played an important role in his self-education as a student at a school of architecture that had abandoned classical teaching.
13 Chambers, 28.
14 David Watkin, *Sir John Soane: Enlightenment Thought and the Royal Academy Lectures* (Cambridge: Cambridge University Press, 1996), lecture II, 504.
15 Jean-Nicolas-Louis Durand, *Précis des leçons d'architecture* (Paris: Ecole Polytechnique, 1802), vol. I, 29 and 30.
16 David Watkin, *The Life and Work of C. R. Cockerell* (London: Zwemmer, 1974), chap. 1.
17 Edward Croft-Murray, *Decorative Painting in England 1537–1837*, 2 vols. (London: Country Life, 1970), vol. II, 190, pls. 115–16.
18 David Watkin, *The Classical Country House: From the Archives of Country Life* (London: Aurum Press, 2009), 76–81.
19 One wall of this room was re-erected in the Victoria and Albert Museum, London, when the house was demolished in c. 1934. See Croft-Murray, loc. cit., 274, pl. 118.
20 See *Roomscape: The Decorative Architecture of Renzo Mongiardino* (New York: Rizzoli, 2001).
21 The quotations from Owen Jones, *The Grammar of Ornament* (London: Day & Son, 1856), are from pp. 5, 2, and 13.

CHAPTER SEVEN
PROPORTIONS OF INTERIORS
1 Leonardo Fibonacci (c. 1170–c. 1250), an Italian mathematician, in his book *Liber Abaci* (1202) popularized the use of Arabic numerals in Europe and introduced a number sequence in which each number is the sum of the previous two. The ratio of two adjacent numbers approaches the "golden ratio." The beginning of the sequence is 0, 1, 1, 2, 3, 5, 8, 13, 21 . . .
2 Edge elements include cornices, baseboards, and door casings.

INDEX

ILLUSTRATION CREDITS